DE VILLE PRESTIGE

More slender than ever before, the Third Generation of the De Ville Prestige has been introduced with all the emblematic DNA you'd expect, but with a comprehensive upgrade across the design. This new 40 mm model in stainless steel and 18K Sedna™ Gold is presented on a modernised Prestige bracelet. The domed silvery dial offers a crystal finish, along with Roman numerals and cabochon indexes, while on the inside, the Co-Axial Master Chronometer calibre ensures unrivalled accuracy at all hours of the day.

D1579743

V1 Kitchen

VIPP.COM

vipp

COMING SOON
A world of outstanding natural beauty

Immerse yourself in the thrill of the wild with this collection of 18 new travel stories from *Kinfolk*. Whatever your pace or purpose, *Kinfolk Wilderness* brings together inspiring itineraries from the full breadth of the planet that promise adventure, inspire awe and spark a deeper connection to the landscape.

Pre-order now at Kinfolk.com

KINFOLK

MAGAZINE

—

EDITOR IN CHIEF	John Burns
EDITOR	Harriet Fitch Little
ART DIRECTOR	Christian Møller Andersen
DESIGN DIRECTOR	Alex Hunting
COPY EDITOR	Rachel Holzman
DESIGN ASSISTANT	Joseph Sinclair Parker

STUDIO

—

PUBLISHING DIRECTOR	Edward Mannering
STUDIO & PROJECT MANAGER	Susanne Buch Petersen
DESIGNER & ART DIRECTOR	Staffan Sundström
DIGITAL MANAGER	Cecilie Jegsen

—

CROSSWORD	Mark Halpin
PUBLICATION DESIGN	Alex Hunting Studio
COVER PHOTOGRAPH	Michael Oliver Love

WORDS

—

Precious Adesina
Allyssia Alleyne
Alex Anderson
Ellie Austin
Annabel Bai Jackson
Louise Benson
Louise Bruton
Ed Cumming
Stephanie d'Arc Taylor
Daphnée Denis
Hadani Ditmars
Marah Eakin
Marianne Eloise
Tom Faber
Robert Ito
Rosalind Jana
Tal Janner-Klausner
Farah-Silvana Kanaan
Jenna Mahale
Okechukwu Nzelu
Agnish Ray
Asher Ross
George Upton
Alice Vincent
Salome Wagaine
Annick Weber

STYLING, SET DESIGN,
HAIR & MAKEUP

—

Denis Bjerregaard
Tine Daring
Ludivine François
Avery Golson
Inga Hewett
Chloe Hicks
Yumiko Hikage
Lisa Jahovic
Malene Kirkegaard
Camilla Larsson
Camille Lichtenstern
Mandy Nash
Lasse Pedersen
Ivy Quan
Giulia Querenghi
Déborah Sadoun
Zinn Zhou

ARTWORK &
PHOTOGRAPHY

—

Sissel Abel
Lauren Bamford
Sergiy Barchuk
Ted Belton
Laurent Boullard
Luc Braquet
Henrik Bülow
William Bunce
Justin Chung
Cayce Clifford
Marina Denisova
Ryan Duffin
Yasmina Gonin
Cecilie Jegsen
Anish Kapoor
Kourtney Kyung Smith
Brigitte Lacombe
Bastien Lattanzio
Romain Laurent
Michael Oliver Love
Rami Mansour
Sabine Marcelis
Katie McCurdy
Ye Rin Mok
Pascal Moscheni
Charles Negre
Corey Olsen
Samuel Pasquier
Martin Pauer
Paul Taggart
Neige Thébault
Emma Trim
Gioncarlo Valentine
Julien Vallon
Jos Wheeler
Gustav Willeit
Xiaopeng Yuan

PUBLISHER

—

Chul-Joon Park

The views expressed in *Kinfolk* magazine are those of the respective contributors and are not necessarily shared by the company or its staff. *Kinfolk* (ISSN 2596-6154) is published quarterly by Ouur ApS, Amagertorv 14B, 2, 1160 Copenhagen, Denmark. Printed by Park Communications Ltd in London, United Kingdom. Color reproduction by Park Communications Ltd in London, United Kingdom. All rights reserved. No part of this publication may be reproduced, distributed or transmitted in any form or by any means, including photocopying or other electronic or mechanical methods, without prior written permission of the editor in chief, except in the case of brief quotations embodied in critical reviews and certain other noncommercial uses permitted by copyright law. The US annual subscription price is $80 USD. Airfreight and mailing in the USA by WN Shipping USA, 156-15, 146th Avenue, 2nd Floor, Jamaica, NY 11434, USA. Application to mail at periodicals postage prices is pending at Jamaica NY 11431. US Postmaster: Send address changes to *Kinfolk*, WN Shipping USA, 156-15, 146th Avenue, 2nd Floor, Jamaica, NY 11434, USA. Subscription records are maintained at Ouur ApS, Amagertorv 14B, 2, 1160 Copenhagen, Denmark. SUBSCRIBE: *Kinfolk* is published four times a year. To subscribe, visit kinfolk.com/subscribe or email us at info@kinfolk.com. CONTACT US: If you have questions or comments, please write to us at info@kinfolk.com. For advertising and partnership inquiries, get in touch at advertising@kinfolk.com.

HOUSE OF FINN JUHL

Our Philosophy

Since we started manufacturing furniture 32 years ago, more than 400 furniture workshops have disappeared from Denmark. Many companies have outsourced their production to places with cheaper labor. These circumstances, together with the Danish society's interest for academic education, have starved the otherwise honored Danish furniture production and education of skilled craftspeople.

We are committed to work against this development.

Still today, the largest part of our Finn Juhl collection is produced in Denmark with a few, selected wooden frames proudly produced in Japan.

This year, we made the acquisition of another Danish workshop in order to expand our Danish production even further. For us, it is crucial that the highest level of craftmanship is also to be found in Denmark in the future.

H F J

Discover more about our philosophy at finnjuhl.com

WELCOME
The Well-being Issue

The question of what constitutes a life well-lived has been *Kinfolk*'s fundamental inquiry for over a decade of publication. For spring, we are embracing the season of rejuvenation with a special issue dedicated to well-being.

Before we go further, allow us to clarify: Well-being is not to be confused with notions of wellness. Whereas well-being suggests a general harmony between body, soul and mind, the word *wellness* has come to encompass an industry dedicated to the constant quest for self-optimization, often through costly interventions. As a primer on the subject, you may wish to begin with the essay "Too Much of a Good Thing" on page 134, in which writer Annabel Bai Jackson warns of how the scales can easily tip toward obsession. "The purgative, controlling language of toxic wellness —*shred, tone, purify, cleanse*—is anathema to the occasional excess, risk and pleasure that often lead to a more holistically positive life experience," she writes.

Rather than advocating for any particular miracle cure, Issue Forty-Seven promotes the idea of well-being as an innate balance that should be safeguarded. In our themed section, which is subdivided into chapters on the body and the mind, you'll meet inspiring people for whom the well-being of others is paramount: On page 140, we hear from Walt Odets, a clinical psychologist in Berkeley who has been offering men a road map through gay life for over 35 years. We also meet two women, Chani Nicholas and Sonya Passi, whose radical approach to employment—an $80,000 salary floor, unlimited vacation and a wealth-building stipend—proposes a new benchmark for workplace well-being. Other stories include a fashion editorial themed around the benefits of friendship, a conversation with a leading light of the new sobriety movement, Julia Bainbridge, and an interview with dancer Alice Sheppard, who speaks about the potential of movement to transform a person's relationship with their body.

Elsewhere, this issue is full of essays, photography and collaborations that seek to surprise and delight. It includes interviews with several people whose impactful work is conducted away from the public gaze: a sought-after sensitivity reader, the US's most influential weddings editor and a tattoo artist whose LA studio address is a closely guarded secret.

We hope you find these stories as interesting to read as we did to produce and that *Kinfolk* can play a small part in helping you find moments of calm and—dare we say it—well-being, amid the busyness of the everyday.

WORDS
JOHN BURNS
HARRIET FITCH LITTLE

CRAFTED WITH CARE

Simplicity and natural materials are at the heart of Hans J. Wegner's iconic furniture designs. His sense of detail and willingness to rethink design led to iconic pieces free from passing trends but made to last for generations. The elegant CH46 and CH47 dining chairs from 1966, which exemplifies Wegner's ability to staying relevant for the future, are carefully crafted by the skilled woodworkers at Carl Hansen & Søn in Funen, Denmark.

Explore more at CARLHANSEN.COM
or visit your nearest Flagship Store

CARL HANSEN & SØN

16 — 46

STARTERS
On weddings, death and silence.

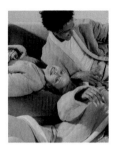

16	Word: Döstädning	33	Age Appropriation
18	What's the Matter?	34	Street Levels
19	That's Life	36	Simone Bodmer-Turner
20	Jean Touitou	38	Draw the Line
24	Rhythm Doctor	40	Veneda Carter
26	The Brand Wagon	42	Minor Miracles
28	Forget It	44	Thanks, I Hate It
30	Charanna Alexander	45	The Friendship Paradox
32	Second Thoughts	46	How to Change a Name

48 — 112

FEATURES
Friendship, furniture and tattoos.

48	Farida Khelfa	84	Home Tour: Vill'Alcina
58	Hot Desk	96	Essay: Holier Than Thou
68	Dr. Woo	100	Between Us
74	Preview: *Kinfolk Wilderness*	—	—

"When I read what I lived through, I think it's crazy." (Farida Khelfa – P. 50)

Photo: Michael Oliver Love

"Loneliness told people where they needed to go." (Julia Bainbridge – P. 133)

114 — 176

WELL-BEING
A check-in for body and mind.

Part I: The Body
116 Dancing with Alice Sheppard
126 Sobriety with Julia Bainbridge
134 Essay: Too Much of a Good Thing
—   —

Part II: The Mind
140 Therapy with Walt Odets
150 Chani Nicholas and Sonya Passi
158 Wild Nights and Duvet Days
168 A Picture of Health

178 — 192

DIRECTORY
An artist, an architect and a crossword.

178 Peer Review
179 Object Matters
180 Cult Rooms
182 Rachid Koraïchi
184 Behind the Scenes
186 Crossword

187 Correction
189 Last Night
190 Credits
191 Stockists
192 My Favorite Thing
—   —

Photo: Emma Trim

marset
Taking care of light

16 — 46

STARTERS
On memories, miracles and poetry.

16	Word: Döstädning	33	Age Appropriation
18	What's the Matter?	34	Street Levels
19	That's Life	36	Simone Bodmer-Turner
20	Jean Touitou	38	Draw the Line
24	Rhythm Doctor	40	Veneda Carter
26	The Brand Wagon	42	Minor Miracles

WORD: DÖSTÄDNING
A Swedish solution to the mess of death.

Etymology: In 2018, author and artist Margareta Magnusson hit *The New York Times* bestseller list with her book *The Gentle Art of Swedish Death Cleaning*. Although it might sound like a service performed at a Stockholm crime scene, death cleaning, or "döstädning" in Swedish, actually refers to the art of decluttering prior to one's own demise. The word is a simple portmanteau, coined by Magnusson, of "dö" (death) and "städning" (cleaning). It takes its place alongside a myriad of other systems—the KonMari Method most famous among them —that promise to turn the arduous task of getting rid of stuff into a streamlined process.[1]

Meaning: Although the word may have been brought to the mainstream by Magnusson, it refers to a culturally established practice of sorting and downsizing that also serves as a form of legacy-shaping. Anyone who has ever cleared out an elderly relative's house after their death is acutely aware of the literal and symbolic weight of things left behind. Whether endless photo albums or closets holding the intimate remnants of a life—from kitchen pans to bags full of mysterious wires—such clearances often demand huge amounts of time and decision-making (and trips to Goodwill with donations).

Magnusson's method encourages a forward-thinking approach to our accumulated possessions. She suggests that instead of shying away from death, we engage with it forthrightly: choosing the objects we actively want to pass on to friends and family, and those that would be better to say goodbye to now. It's a win-win situation. You get all the satisfaction of paring back your life, sifting through important memories and focusing on the things you really value, while loved ones will be grateful to avoid the posthumous sorting of your baseball card collection. It may even help you come to grips with some of the natural fears and anxieties surrounding mortality.

Although Magnusson recommends this approach for those who are at a stage of life where death is getting closer, it can be a clarifying method for anyone who wants to thoughtfully winnow the contents of their home. Magnusson's practical steps include first tackling items that are stored out of sight (boxes stashed in an attic, for example), ditching anything that might be hurtful to discover, slowly regifting precious things while you're alive, keeping a list of passwords for family to access important data and saving photos, letters and other sentimental items until last so you can process them properly.

(1) Other organizational methods popularized in recent years include the FlyLady method (declutter in short bursts, using a timer), the Peter Walsh method (remove *everything* from the room first) and the Colleen Madsen method (remove one thing a day for 365 days).

WORDS
ROSALIND JANA
PHOTO
JULIEN VALLON

17

Maybe it's the pandemic or maybe it's because, for the last seven or so years, it's felt like society is constantly on the cusp of complete collapse, but it seems like we've become desensitized to other people's personal issues.

That's not to say that some things don't hit home. Everyone feels terrible for disaster victims, grieving families and those who are struggling with other obvious tragedies. The wackier worries can spark interest, too: When a friend recently recounted how she was dealing with a seven-year-old son who wants to be naked every minute he's home, even if other people are in the house, I felt genuinely sorry, telling her very seriously that I had no idea how I'd deal with that hellacious (and hilarious) issue.

But when faced with more common daily woes—your garden-variety fender benders, battles with insomnia, lost wallets or even mild bouts of identity theft—it's become all too commonplace to nod soberly and offer mild condolences. They'll get over it.

Why are some problems more apt to elicit sympathy while others draw a collective shrug, and how can we all get better at caring about someone else's concerns, no matter what they are? It all comes down to empathy and ego, most likely. It's easy to quickly gloss over others' problems—especially if we've handily dealt with something similar on our own. That quickly diminishes their experiences, though, and makes them feel like the issue that's plaguing their lives—whether it's anxiety, a low bank balance or a long-lingering cough—doesn't really deserve to take up our precious brain space.

It's worth remembering that while a friend's troubles might seem like small potatoes to you, they can be absolutely world-destroying to the sufferer. If someone is concerned enough about an issue to raise it in a discussion, it's worth your consideration and sympathy. After all, every problem merits compassion, no matter whether you happen to think it's a mountain or a molehill.

WORDS
MARAH EAKIN
PHOTO
PASCAL MOSCHENI

WHAT'S THE MATTER?
On the struggle to care equally.

Model: Miranda Makaroff

In the toughest of times or during the most difficult conversations, the impulse is often to search for convenient expressions that make a situation feel more manageable. "It is what it is!" "It could be worse!" "Damned if you do, damned if you don't!"

These seemingly uplifting platitudes—which can bring even the most heated discussion to a dead stop—are called "thought-terminating clichés." The term was popularized in 1961 by American psychiatrist and author Robert Jay Lifton. In *Thought Reform and the Psychology of Totalism*, Lifton wrote that, with thought-terminating clichés, "The most far-reaching and complex of human problems are compressed into brief, highly reductive, definitive-sounding phrases."

These apparently positive expressions can make complex emotions easily digestible while offering little room for reflection. In *Cultish*, American author and linguist Amanda Montell points to QAnon, the internet conspiracy theory, using phrases such as "trust the plan" or "do your research" as a case in which clichés are used to shut down conversation. Telling someone to do their research insinuates that they are not knowledgeable enough to make up their own mind—or even to discuss the topic further. Consequently, thought-terminating clichés can be a highly dangerous tool of rhetoric. The philosopher and Holocaust survivor Hannah Arendt wrote in *The New Yorker* in 1963 that Otto Adolf Eichmann, one of the primary organizers of the Holocaust, "was genuinely incapable of uttering a single sentence that was not a cliché."

Of course, sometimes a phrase that shuts down thought can serve positive ends. Alcoholics Anonymous and charity fundraising campaigns use similar language to encourage and unify their community. In *Alcoholics Anonymous: Cult or Cure?*, author Charles Bufe writes that "thought-stopping phrases include any use of language, especially repeated phrases, to ward off forbidden thoughts." A saying such as "take each day one step at a time" might be trite, but it can acquire a mantra-like quality for those struggling. Sometimes a phrase that grants permission to stop overthinking isn't a get-out-of-jail-free card, it's a lifeline.

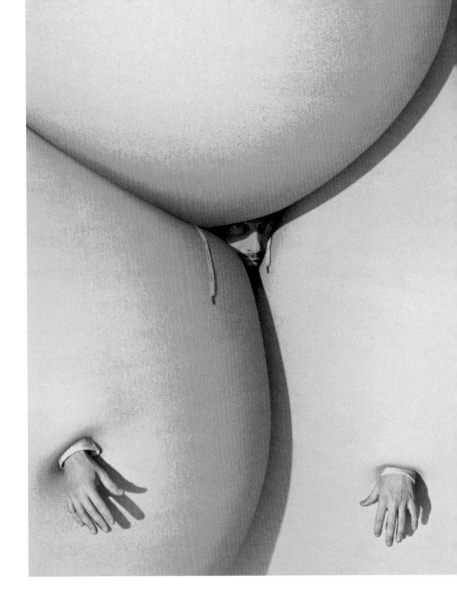

WORDS
PRECIOUS ADESINA
PHOTO
ROMAIN LAURENT

THAT'S LIFE
The quiet tyranny of clichés.

JEAN TOUITOU

WORDS
ANNICK WEBER

The A.P.C. founder on the demands of hype and craft.

"Leave me alone and let me do exactly what I want to do." Few brands would release such a statement for their 35th anniversary, but coming from Jean Touitou—the founder of A.P.C.—it's perhaps less of a surprise. Since launching his clothing label in Paris in 1987, the entrepreneur has changed the way we consume fashion, giving the world a wardrobe built on chic staples rather than trends. It is as though, in refusing to play by the industry's rule book, Touitou has changed it: Much of what other brands preach today—a less-is-more ethos, the use of natural materials and a penchant for clean, gender-defying cuts—has always been part of the A.P.C. story.

In his label's 35-year-long history, Touitou has collaborated with everyone from American work wear giant Carhartt WIP to the 1970s style icon Jane Birkin and has opened 102 stand-alone boutiques. But A.P.C. remains fiercely independent. Apart from one minority investor, Touitou is the sole stakeholder in the company. At 71, he has no plan to retire, let alone sell A.P.C. "It seems like we don't live on the same planet," he says of luxury conglomerates. "When you have a bestseller, all they want to do is to invade the world with it." Touitou prefers keeping things at a manageable scale as it gives him the most important freedom of all: being left to do what he wants.

ANNICK WEBER: Where did the idea to start A.P.C. come from?

JEAN TOUITOU: It sounds like a fairy tale, but it was when my suitcase got lost on a trip to Barcelona. I realized I couldn't find a pair of jeans in the shops. They were all selling washed denim; there was no way I would wear something like this. That's when I realized I should make what I couldn't find myself.

AW: So no-fuss materials like raw denim have always been key to the brand?

JT: Yes. For the raw denim I work with a factory in Japan—I think we're only three people in the world to know the secret behind it. I've also been using a lot of military fabrics from the start. Work wear and streetwear are a big inspiration—plus the idea that things should fit everybody. I've always made some sort of androgynous fashion.

AW: Why did you branch out from making the jeans that A.P.C. was once best known for?

JT: Just look at the record industry; it's now completely dead because it followed the wrong recipe in the 1990s. You could have had a huge summer hit, and then the marketing team would say, "Okay, let's write a song with the same beat and it will work again." But it doesn't; it becomes boring.

AW: How do you keep things from becoming boring now that A.P.C. is so established as an all-around fashion brand?

JT: We don't do crazy stuff, but we do stuff that has a lot of personality. We had a show in Paris which none of the press was interested in. We used students from my daughter's class, who was 17 at the time. There was no casting director saying "You're too tall or you're too large." Everyone who wanted to do the show could do it. I almost cried that day, it was such a generous idea. I thought it was genius, not the fashion necessarily, but the fact that we had no models.

AW: What do you think sets you apart from other fashion makers?

JT: I'm not buying influencers or making flashy things, I'm not

Opposite Photo: Bastien Lattanzio. Overleaf Photo: Brigitte Lacombe

playing that game. Still, I do believe that in all those years, I've been doing nothing but fashion—very advanced fashion even. I know that because I see people in the streets and notice that I'm helping them be prouder of themselves for the way they look. I'm happy to belong to that industry with my own perception of it.

AW: What has been the biggest shift in the way A.P.C. operates?

JT: We've just been ourselves. Some fashion brands prefer burning their pieces from past collections than selling them with a discount, for example. They think it hurts their image. I don't think I'm hurting the image of my brand by doing that; I'm glad that we have APC Surplus stores in all major cities. The thing with A.P.C. is that you can still wear old pieces with no shame because we are less affected by this permanent change in fashion.

AW: Inspiring people to consume less . . . doesn't this contradict the raison d'être of any business?

JT: I think more brands will go that way. People are starting to want to buy less and to go back to quality and durability. And maybe people are getting tired of fashion as a sign of social status. They are no longer looking for these big luxury labels that are branding themselves too much.

AW: How do you feel about the idea of your clothes as status symbols?

JT: I have to compromise. We use logos occasionally; we found out that a plain white T-shirt doesn't sell so well, even if you explain to people that it's produced from the best cotton.

AW: Your wife, Judith, is A.P.C.'s artistic director. How do you navigate work and life?

JT: It's like a ménage à trois: There's her, me and A.P.C. It's part of our life. Mostly it's her coming up with good ideas, I make the idea better and she'll make it even better. Judith is more into the collections. She works more than me; it's my privilege of age. I'm not in the design meetings, but I'm still part of the strategy. Our collective works well.

AW: What about your staff? Where do they come in?

JT: It took me 35 years to hire my teams at design, image and finance. I feel like I'm the manager of the Rolling Stones, the Beatles, the Doors, the Velvet Underground and Pink Floyd. I have golden people with me. *They* are the creators of A.P.C. I can say that the collections are getting better and better; we are able to open six stores a year; and still, everyone goes home at 6:30. We're not one of those fashion brands that feels more comfortable when everyone goes home at midnight.

AW: Is there anything you wish you had done differently?

JT: I wish I could go back to 1993 and spend three months in our Mercer Street store and look at all these people coming there. Because that's where the mythology of A.P.C. started, in New York, more than in Paris. It's like a handsome person who's looking at a picture from the past and saying to themselves, "Gee, I was looking so good."

RHYTHM DOCTOR
The pacifying effect of poetry.

The American poet Robert Frost once said that "the surest way to reach the heart is through the ear." As he told journalist Sterling Brown in 1936, "the visual images thrown up by a poem are important, but it is more important still to choose and arrange words in a sequence so as virtually to control the intonation and pauses of the reader's voice."

Frost was speaking about the heart as the source of emotions, but it seems it is possible to take him literally as well: Studies have shown that reading poetry aloud can slow your heart rate, while also reducing stress and increasing feelings of well-being. It is an effect that Sir Jonathan Bate, the Foundation Professor of Environmental Humanities at Arizona State University, compares to beta-blockers, drugs that prevent the buildup of adrenaline in stressful situations.

The phenomenon in itself is nothing new. Plato wrote in the fourth century B.C. about the rhapsodes, professional performers of Greek poetry, being induced into a trancelike state when reciting epic poems like Homer's *Odyssey*. Plato, however, lacked the modern-day technology to measure breathing rate and heart rate variability (HRV—the degree to which your heart rate fluctuates). Researchers have found that as well as regulating your HRV, reading poetry aloud can cause your breathing to synchronize with your heartbeat, a similar indicator of well-being. So next time you know you're likely to find yourself in a stressful situation, why not follow Bate's advice and bring along a book of poetry?

WORDS
GEORGE UPTON
PHOTO
SAMUEL PASQUIER

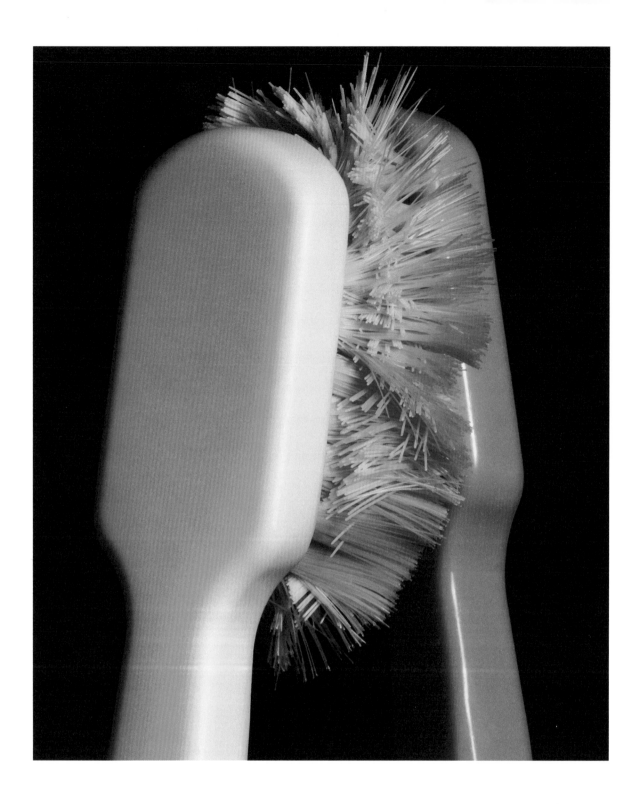

26

Set Design: Camille Lichtenstern

THE BRAND WAGON
When good collaborations go bad.

WORDS
ALLYSSIA ALLEYNE
PHOTO
YASMINA GONIN

There was a time when brand partnerships—your Rodarte for Target and Hermès for Bugatti—felt rare and noteworthy. But now, every season brings with it a slew of unlikely bedfellows: Reebok and *National Geographic*; Burberry and Minecraft; Juicy Couture and Kraft Mayo. There's no pairing too incongruous in the age of memes.

This cross-pollination is big business. A 2021 Statista study found that 67% of Gen Z and 60% of millennials reported purchasing co-branded products and that 71% of American consumers feel positive about such collaborations. Done well, they're a way for companies to widen their audiences and generate sales, while sharing the costs and risks. Done poorly, they can inflict serious reputational damage, alienating new and existing customers alike.[1]

Let's take for granted that all corporate activities, concerned as they are with buyers and bottom lines, are driven by profit. The best collaborations should convince you they're driven by something deeper. In 2019, followers of fashion couldn't help but be charmed when Belgian designer Dries Van Noten and the retired grand couturier Christian Lacroix came together for a one-off collection that combined the former's practical luxury with the latter's trademark frills. *The New York Times* fashion critic Vanessa Friedman described it as "a reminder that at its purest, creative collaboration is a meeting of the eyes and the minds" rather than "the most naked form of mutual back scratching."

Often, however, collaborations are less an exchange of ideas between equals than a game of clout by association—think of Supreme trading street cred for luxury bona fides in its collabs with Tiffany and Louis Vuitton, or Van Noten's own upcoming Stüssy capsule. Christie's tried for a similar trick last fall when it released a line of merch emblazoned with the words "Art Handler" with streetwear site Highsnobiety.

But edginess isn't so easily transposed. The auction house was swiftly slammed for trivializing the poor working conditions of art handlers within their own business. The collaboration was shelved after a single day and Christie's apologized.

Safer, then, to stay in your lane, to give the people what they actually want. This is why Justin Bieber's limited-edition line of "Timbiebs Timbits" donut holes with Canadian café chain Tim Hortons made sense. It may be hard to take the singer seriously when he says "Doing a Tim Hortons collab had always been a dream of mine." But there's something authentic about two mass-market brands creating something their mutual fan base might genuinely enjoy, at a price point they can afford. If it was silly, at least everyone involved seemed to be in on the joke. The collaboration paid off: Bieber was credited with almost single-handedly turning around the chain's fortunes, leading to a 10.3% rise in sales at stores open at least a year in the fourth quarter of 2021.

The Dries–Lacroix collection never had quite the same commercial impact. Hitting stores in spring 2020, as people tightened their purse strings and pulled on their sweatpants, the collection flooded Net-a-Porter's sales section later the same year. If the designers are to be believed, this shouldn't be taken as a failure. Like the most satisfying collaborations, brand or otherwise, this was organic and special—a case of two people driven to explore the limits of what they could make together, rather than how much they could make doing it.

(1) The half-century relationship between Shell and Lego, which involved the plastic bricks being distributed in gas stations around the world, came to an end in 2014 after a successful Greenpeace campaign that ran with the tagline "Shell is polluting our kids' imagination."

FORGET IT
The problem with core memories.

Artwork: *Perkra* by Gustav Willeit

Coined by the 2015 Pixar film *Inside Out*, "core memories" are rare, vivid experiences that stay with us all our lives. In the film, core memories are portrayed as glowing orbs that are filed deep within the protagonist's consciousness, forming the essence of who she is. When she loses them, she loses herself.

Now, core memories have emerged as a hit theme on TikTok. Popular videos show brothers and sisters jumping into the ocean for the first time, sudden rainstorms after soccer games, babies and puppies sharing tubs of ice cream. And many of the videos come with a message of encouragement: Get outside and make some memories!

The trouble is that core memories—at least as they are portrayed in *Inside Out*—are not a real psychological phenomenon. Seemingly important experiences often fade from our minds, and oddly minor ones stick. Just ask the parent who films their family dancing in the Louvre courtyard on vacation, only to find their kids don't remember a thing except for those fantastic airport hand dryers.

Still, 880 million TikTok users can't be all wrong. Sure, we forget many of our experiences in life, but most of us do retain a handful of special memories that never seem to lose their clarity and emotional reality. These memories likely embed during moments of strong emotion; joy, early romantic yearnings, high-voltage embarrassment. And we discover more and more meaning within them as time passes.

Let's imagine one: A woman remembers herself as a child. It's summertime. She opens the front door, and there in the driveway is her favorite aunt ringing a bicycle bell. It's a gift! The aunt smiles and yells "Come and try it!" The afternoon seems impossibly full of light. It feels *wonderful*. For years this is the whole of the memory, and then one day a new layer is revealed. Now the woman realizes her memory is all about joy in contrast with what else was going on at the time. The aunt had arrived against the backdrop of her parents' divorce. How hadn't she remembered that before? The house had been full of anger and accusation. And then, on that special day, light and safety came pouring in. Later still, when the aunt has passed away, the memory returns. Now the woman realizes how perfectly it condenses all that she loved about her. All of who she was is painted in the memory of her smile, the bell and that wonderful, freeing shout: "Come and try it!"

Among neurologists and psychologists, consensus suggests that remembering is a constructive process. We do not simply request a file and examine it upon delivery. Instead, our hippocampus gathers elements of the memory—what we saw, what we smelled, what we felt—from different brain regions. In reassembling these partial elements, we inevitably inflect the memory with new aspects based on our current needs, insights and fears. When we do this we reinforce the memory, raking the leaves from the neural pathways that lead to it, making it stronger even as we modify it.

It's a confusing business. What allows one beautiful experience to fall out of our mind in a matter of weeks, while another embeds and matures over a lifetime? Only one thing is certain: We can't force good memories into existence any easier than we can forget the worst of them.

WORDS
ASHER ROSS
ARTWORK
GUSTAV WILLEIT

CHARANNA ALEXANDER

WORDS
ELLIE AUSTIN
PHOTOS
GIONCARLO VALENTINE

Five questions for a professional romantic.

Charanna Alexander is paid to read love stories. As *The New York Times*' Weddings editor, she sifts through submissions from couples across America who want their nuptials to be immortalized in print, a custom that began in September 1851 when the newspaper published one single-line wedding announcement in its first-ever edition. Traditionally considered the preserve of high-society figures with enviable lives, the paper's Weddings section has served as inspiration for comedy sketches, a parody Twitter account and *Sex and the City* dialogue (Carrie Bradshaw described it as "the single woman's sports pages"). In recent years, however, there's been a shift away from an emphasis on social standing to a focus on diverse relationships and less traditional love stories.

ELLIE AUSTIN: What are you looking for when you read through applications from couples?

CHARANNA ALEXANDER: I'm always looking for a larger theme. Recently, we featured a couple where the groom was in an accident that left him quadriplegic. The bride hadn't heard from him and thought she was being ghosted until a friend reached out and said, "He's in the hospital fighting for his life." The groom rebuilding his life was part of their love story. These people have wonderful, interesting jobs. They are, I would say, well-to-do. But that story really struck a chord with me about resilience. I want somebody to read ⌊the announcement⌋ and say, "Wow, that was powerful," or "I can't believe a love or situation like that exists."

EA: What happens once a couple is chosen?

CA: We ask people to submit applications six weeks prior to their wedding date. Our reporters contact them asking for an available date for an interview. Then, it's rigorous fact-checking—from where they went to school to the restaurant they ate at for their first date. I think the couples we feature are incredibly brave because of the scrutiny.

EA: Can you elaborate?

CA: We recently featured a couple who met in a parking lot during the pandemic. It was not received well on Twitter in that many people bashed the bride for giving the groom a second and third opportunity to start a relationship. My answer to that is we're not looking for fairy-tale weddings because love is messy. It isn't always linear.

EA: Do people go to surprising lengths to be featured?

CA: One of my reporters was invited to a wedding in Fiji, all expenses paid. I've been offered box seats at a New York Yankees game. Obviously, we can't accept. Generally, people respect that this is a sacred part of the paper and they can't buy their way into it.

EA: Is there a love story that you haven't told yet but want to?

CA: There are communities that are deeply spiritual that have beliefs outside of any of the religions that are mainly talked about. I would love to see if there's some kind of flame ceremony in a forest or ⌊a ceremony⌋ where a couple walks into an ocean as a symbolic way of joining themselves in marriage. I'm seeking those unique ways that people are committing themselves that don't necessarily look like we know.

When basking in the glory of a breath-taking debut, it can be difficult to imagine that it may ever be otherwise. But what comes up must come down. "Second album syndrome" is a whispered curse in the music industry, born of the theory that artists spend short lifetimes pouring their creative energies into a debut album, only to have to match that success with a second one bashed out in the midst of life-changing fame, touring and great expectation.

Famous examples of the sophomore slump include *Room on Fire*, the rather predictable follow-up to the Strokes' genre-changing debut, *Is This It?*, the Stone Roses' underwhelming *Second Coming* and the Who's not-hasty-enough *A Quick One*. But the same rule applies even to Queen Bey. Beyoncé's first solo album, *Dangerously in Love*, remains her best-selling. She followed in the footsteps of Whitney and Britney, whose debuts are still their most commercially successful.

Second album syndrome can filter into normal life, too. There's the stress that only becomes apparent after a particularly good first six months in a new job, for instance. Or the persistent work necessary to nurture a burgeoning friendship when the thrill of mutual infatuation dissipates. It's relatively easy to enjoy initial success in something we didn't hold high expectations for, but it's far harder to maintain it for the long haul.

Consider that the pressure put on a second album is relatively modern: 50 years ago, artists were given time to flex their creative muscle; *Pet Sounds* was the Beach Boys' *ninth* record. Perhaps we shouldn't see our first attempt at something as necessarily being our best ever, but simply the best we could do at the time. And then we can be confident that we will grow and develop once we have gained that experience. Jeff Buckley, who sadly died with just one masterpiece-worthy album to his name, offered the following insight: "If you feel blocked, do not turn to others, but look inside, in silence, for the enemy of your progress."

WORDS
ALICE VINCENT
PHOTO
LAUREN BAMFORD

SECOND THOUGHTS
The ubiquity of second album syndrome.

Photo: Courtesy of House Editions

AGE APPROPRIATION
When actors don't act their age.

WORDS
ROBERT ITO
PHOTO
CHARLES NEGRE

In the HBO series *Euphoria*, Zendaya delivers a bravura performance as Rue Bennett, a 17-year-old high school student and recovering drug addict. Zendaya's performance is all the more remarkable because she has never used drugs—not even booze—nor did she have a typical high school experience, whatever that might be, having been a celebrity since she was a teen. She's also 26, a bit long in the tooth for a high school junior. Or is she? Certainly not in TV shows or movies, where it's fairly common for actors to play teenagers well into their 20s and even 30s. In case you've forgotten any of them—like Andrew Garfield's turn as a teenage Spider-Man (27!), Stacey Dash as Dionne Davenport in *Clueless* (28!) or Stockard Channing playing Betty Rizzo in Grease (33!)—there are numerous online lists with headlines like "30 Actors Who Played Teenagers When They Were Super Old" to refresh your memory.

There are several good reasons for this longstanding practice. Minors can only work so many hours a day due to child labor laws, and usually require tutors or guardians on set. Teen actors often can't do the sorts of sex scenes that a grown-up

actor could (even when that grown-up is playing a teen having sex). Teens get acne. And actors in their 20s and 30s are often simply better actors than they were in their teens, take Zendaya, for instance.

Of course, there are all sorts of downsides to the practice, including how real teens, at the height of their adolescent gawkiness, might feel about seeing themselves played by gorgeous, smooth-skinned actors who have had the time to grow out of their own gawky phases. Feeling good about your looks is tough enough for 13-year-olds without having to compete with these "peers."

There probably isn't a way out of this, unless all the studios collectively decide to follow the lead of franchises like *Harry Potter* and *Stranger Things* and hire only kids to play kids, a practice that worked for those two series largely because many of the characters were supposed to be misfits anyway—and who better than a teen for something like that? Or perhaps a simple disclaimer is in order, something along the lines of "characters on your screen may be older than they appear."

STREET LEVELS
The false promise of a silent city.

WORDS
ANNABEL BAI JACKSON
ARTWORK
ANISH KAPOOR

Click on Japan's Dorozoku website, and a map pockmarked with clusters of orange and yellow circles will appear—each one representing a noisy resident. Invented by a work-from-home software developer in 2016, the digital map allows users to pinpoint spots of sonic disturbance, from squawking children to chatty couples. It serves as a warning to noise-phobes: Enter these zones at your peril.[1]

The map is controversial in Japan, where its exposure of people's daily hubbub is seen as an anonymous shaming ritual. But the Dorozoku platform reveals a silent frustration for unwanted sounds, a discontent that expands out to the cacophony of modernity itself—the whirring cranes that erect the skyline at 5 a.m., the grating thrum of cars whipping down the highway.

In any collective environment, there's a conflict between the space we physically inhabit and the space we sonically inhabit. We expect, to a degree, that the two will align: that our front doors will shield us from trespassers as much as from the sound of boom cars and the neighbor's morning school run. But any absolute boundary is impossible. Noise leaks through apartment walls, bleeds over garden fences and spools in from airplanes, traffic and construction. It undermines the very promises granted by private property: a sovereign space, a room of one's own.

What right to silence do we have, then, if our soundscape is inevitably shared? Auditory disturbance can jeopardize health, with the World Health Organization describing it as an "underestimated threat." But at its extreme, the dream of a silent utopia becomes a full-blown moral panic. Noise Free America, a "coalition" doing battle with noise on all fronts—from airport terminals' Muzak to garden leaf blowers—declares so-called "noise violators" to be "criminally-minded" and intent on "pursu[ing] lawlessness." Lurking inside every toddler there's a potential felon. Here, the right to silence slips into the right to interpret from decibels alone, to clench the fist of social control. Noise is never received neutrally: The exaggerated revving of an engine becomes a sign of machismo, the crying of a child demonstrates a lack of parental discipline.

For the less zealous, a silent city may come with trade-offs. Enforced quiet—imposed, say, through city-wide regulations—is far from a cure-all. Not only would it limit activity and deflate the vitality of urban life, but it would inevitably shrink that third space between home and work. The street—the liminal zone of travel, meetups and play—would be reduced to quiet desolation.

Is there a resolution to the politics of noise? The dissonant tones of cityscapes tend to invoke what cultural theorist Sianne Ngai describes as "ugly feelings"—negative emotions which, in contrast to the dynamic, passionate experiences of joy or rage, assume a minor place in our philosophy of feeling. Urban noise, in particular, inspires these feelings: annoyance rather than anger, irritation rather than rage, quietly dropping pins on an online map instead of screaming at the neighbors. We can overcome our ugly feelings through noise-canceling headphones and gentle neighborly requests; but we can also do so by *listening to*, instead of *overhearing*, the texture of the city—by keeping an ear out for signs of life.

(1) Paris is currently testing sound-detecting speaker and camera systems that identify particularly noisy vehicles such as accelerating motorbikes. A system is due to go into place next year that will issue fines to offending motorists.

Artwork: *Dismemberment, Site I.* © Anish Kapoor / VISDA. Photo: Jos Wheeler

SIMONE BODMER-TURNER

WORDS
PRECIOUS ADESINA
PHOTO
NEIGE THÉBAULT

Meet the artist throwing clay a curveball.

Since California-born sculptor and ceramist Simone Bodmer-Turner opened her studio in Brooklyn in 2018, her distinctively shaped pieces have pushed the boundaries of form, material and practicality. For Bodmer-Turner, creating functional objects out of clay—not just vases, but also chairs, fireplaces and shelving—has been a satisfying challenge. "I don't use it in the way that most people do," she says. "Everybody perceives ceramics as being super fragile, but the clay I use has so much sand in it that it's more like a stone."

In the fall of 2021, Bodmer-Turner relocated from New York to western Massachusetts, allowing her to rekindle her love of ceramics as a natural art form. She's also settled into a smaller scale, making one-off sculptures rather than fashioning vast units. Clay is "one of the most pleasant and calming materials to work with," she says. "But when you're living in the city and ordering premixed clay from a factory, it becomes disjointed."

PRECIOUS ADESINA: A lot of your work is about pushing the boundaries of clay. How do you approach this?

SIMONE BODMER-TURNER: Most people who work with clay think of themselves as potters, but I don't identify with any of the terminology usually applied to people who work with the medium. I use it as if it is some other material, and often people don't realize it's clay. Right now, I'm doing a lot more puzzle piece–like sculptures—multiple parts that fit into each other almost seamlessly.

PA: Shape is a big part of your work, but color seems to be intentionally lacking. Why?

SBT: When I first started moving away from more functional work, I made vases for a long time. I wanted to explore shape, push myself to find my voice and challenge myself to create interesting things, so I stayed away from not necessarily color but glaze. Using glaze in ceramics is a science; there are many ways it can go wrong. I also don't like traditional glaze as it doesn't serve the kind of work that I make. You don't get those sharp lines or shadows in the same way, but with being in Massachusetts and working with more experimental firings, I'm looking forward to exploring surface again. I haven't done that since I worked with wood kilns in Japan.

PA: Why did you shift from design to art?

SBT: I still have the design practice, but I have scaled that back, so it's less business and more art. It's now just one assistant and me working directly with clients. Most of my work is now sculpture or smaller pieces, as requested. Producing at scale was not the right path for me. I was mainly managing the studio, and there wasn't that much time for making my own work.

PA: How has moving from the city to the countryside changed your approach to your work?

SBT: I'm currently splitting my time between Brooklyn and Massachusetts, but I'll be giving up my studio in New York soon. It's one of the hardest decisions I've ever made, but the barn has more space, it is in the middle of a beautiful field and I can build a wood kiln. So there's just a lot more possibility to go in the direction that I want to go in, which is being more in touch with nature and using the natural elements more directly. People are drawn to ceramics because there's this romanticism about working with the earth and having a grounding element to your practice.

DRAW THE LINE
A short history of linear architecture.

In the 1920s, the modern city seemed to hold nothing but promise: order, cleanliness, rapid movement, economic growth and technological progress. But disaffection grew as neatly planned metropolises sprawled and outpaced themselves. In the 1950s, urban planners recommended more order, urban renewal and slum clearances. Dutch artist Constant Nieuwenhuys offered a different alternative in the 1960s: a city of linked megastructures called New Babylon that would drift high over the regimented city and provide a place without order—a place "for playing, for adventure, for mobility."

Since then, plenty of urban planners have taken up the quest to improve our cities. Among the most intriguing strategies is the linear city, an orderly slice of metropolitan energy dominated by a single path of movement. This vaguely recalls agricultural long-lot settlements in which houses and barns, fronting long narrow fields, squeeze together along a single roadway. In linear settlements, neighbors can't help but interact with each other as they go about their lives. They also can't avoid each other. Every interaction becomes more a product of the community's planning than of its people's desires.

The Swiss architect Le Corbusier greatly amplified this linear arrangement in his 1930s design for Algiers. He sought at once to tidy the sprawling city and to command its complex terrain. The Obus ("Shrapnel") Plan would have disrupted everything about the old city. Its most dominant feature was a sinuous highway lifted over the hills on a long wall of housing—residences for 180,000 people overlooking the Mediterranean. Although never built, the urban housing scheme in Algeria anticipated Le Corbusier's influential Unité d'Habitation (Housing Unit), which his firm built on several sites in Europe. It was a long concrete block with hundreds of two-story apartments open to outdoor views but also facing broad interior streets, where people would enjoy chance meetings with their neighbors—an entire city caught up in one building.

The British New Brutalist architects Alison and Peter Smithson expanded this idea of "streets-in-the-air" for public housing projects in London. Their unbuilt Golden Lane design proposed a meandering slab to house 500 people. It promised, they proclaimed, "an infinitely richer and more satisfactory way of living in cities" because people could encounter each other on elevated thoroughfares without ever descending to the surface below. All these plans failed to consider that not all chance meetings are benign, and that mutual confinement does not constitute a community. A built version of the Smithsons' interior streets at Robin Hood Gardens public housing was disastrous, inviting vandalism and crime hidden away from the observant eyes of the city. That building was demolished in 2017.

Hopefully, this will not be the fate of the most audacious linear city project ever attempted: The Line, now under construction in Saudi Arabia. It will be a 105-mile-long conurbation of nine million people, framed by two immense mirrored walls—1,600 feet high and spaced 650 feet apart.[1] The planned reflective shard stretching across mountains and deserts assures "a revolution in civilization" in which "residents will have access to all their daily needs within five-minute walk neighborhoods." That seems a narrow promise. A hundred years of modern sculptural city design suggests that this new linear city may offer little more than geographical constraint, rather than a richly spontaneous, satisfyingly dynamic urban way of life.

(1) The Line has prompted shock and skepticism from many commentators, who see it as unfeasibly ambitious and question the environmental costs of the building and the displacement of tribes in the area. In an appeal to architects who might consider working on the project, published on *Dezeen*, urbanist Adam Greenfield wrote that it was "an ecological and moral atrocity."

WORDS
ALEX ANDERSON
ARTWORK
SABINE MARCELIS

Photo: Rami Mansour

39

VENEDA CARTER

WORDS
ROSALIND JANA
PHOTO
SISSEL ABEL

An interview with a superstar stylist.

Veneda Carter's style is assembled from clashing parts: skewed proportions, billowing fabrics, unexpected details. After growing up in Copenhagen, where she admired her older brother's taste (her teenage soundtrack was heavy on Missy Elliott and Lauryn Hill), the former model caught the eye of Kanye West in 2016 for her boldly layered looks posted to Instagram. A stint as Kim Kardashian's stylist followed, and Carter began working with brands including Stüssy and Timberland. She's a stylist who's always trying to "freak it": ballet flats worn with cargo pants, or heavy boots paired with something delicate.

ROSALIND JANA: What was your first point of contact with the fashion industry?

VENEDA CARTER: I got really into fashion around the same time I started modeling. I was only 13, brought into the industry at a very early age. It introduced me to a world that I had no knowledge of.

RJ: As a model, you're the most visible but you have the least autonomy. Were you interested in styling as a way of having creative control?

VC: One hundred percent. It's such a fulfilling feeling doing something that you're good at, and people appreciating it and wanting more, [especially when] for so many years you didn't feel like you had a say in anything. You were just there—like a product or a mannequin.

RJ: You developed a specific aesthetic—mixing street style with more elegant elements.

VC: I always tried to elevate it because I feel like streetwear is one thing and it's cool for what it is, but I'm still female. I love the tomboy look, and I love baggy clothes, but I always had a mission to flip it or give it a strong feminine perspective.

RJ: You have a knack for tapping into a style that is very much your own, but also seems reflective of wider aesthetic shifts. Do you pay attention to trends?

VC: It is very intuitive with me. I feel like if I looked too much at trends, or what someone is wearing, it would take away my authenticity. I can definitely be inspired by or attracted to elements of what designers are doing, but I always want to make it mine. Right now I'm really into denim, like a capri pant: long, over the knee.

RJ: How do you find it styling yourself versus styling other people? What's it like when you're not using yourself as the canvas?

VC: Sometimes it's easier because I think certain things don't look as good on me. I feel a bit more limited with myself; I can be more experimental when I work with models. There'll be certain ideas that might not [be functional] in real life. When I work on a photo shoot, I have more freedom.

RJ: The fantasy space of fashion imagery is quite separate to the daily realities of personal style. Are there any styling moments that feel particularly memorable to you?

VC: Obviously, my time with Kim [Kardashian] was very special. I learned so much working with her, just exploring my ideas and her being open to a lot. She's one of the most photographed women in the world, so being able to see some of my looks on her, I can't lie, that was a huge moment.

RJ: Are there particular items in your wardrobe that you feel especially proud to own?

VC: I spend a lot of time on eBay. I don't have anything specifically in my closet that I'm like, "Wow," [but] I like to find really rare stuff or even deadstock or old pieces you can't get anymore. I have this one Avirex all-white leather jacket, which I love so much.

MINOR MIRACLES
Why good luck has great odds.

Set Design: Lisa Jahovic

Bill Morgan had already been dubbed Australia's luckiest man when, in 1999, he won the lottery for a second time. The truck driver had been in an accident that left him clinically dead for 14 minutes (twice the time needed to declare someone as having died) and then in a coma for 12 days. Against all odds, Morgan made a miraculous recovery. A year later, after he won a car on a scratch-off lottery ticket, his story caught the attention of national news. Then, while recreating the lucky moment for the cameras, Morgan won again, this time to the tune of 250,000 Australian dollars. What are the chances?!

Well, according to mathematician John Edensor Littlewood, it is not quite as unlikely as you might think. Writing in *A Mathematician's Miscellany* in 1953, Littlewood demonstrated that you can expect to experience an event with the odds of one in a million, which he describes as a "miracle," about once a month. The problem is you just might not notice it. In Littlewood's definition, a "miracle" can be completely random or inconsequential, such as happening to get the last ticket for a music festival or, unbeknownst to you, narrowly avoiding being hit by a bird dropping, twice. Just because they don't have a significant impact on your life, does not mean they are any less remarkable, at least statistically speaking.

We might not always end up better off, but Littlewood's Law shows us how these chance encounters and bizarre coincidences are an everyday part of our lives, and a reminder of how our experience of the world is unique—even if that's just because you are the only person in human history to have won a dollar on the lottery, 10 times in a row. In a way we are all lucky, it's really a matter of perspective.

WORDS
GEORGE UPTON
PHOTO
WILLIAM BUNCE

43

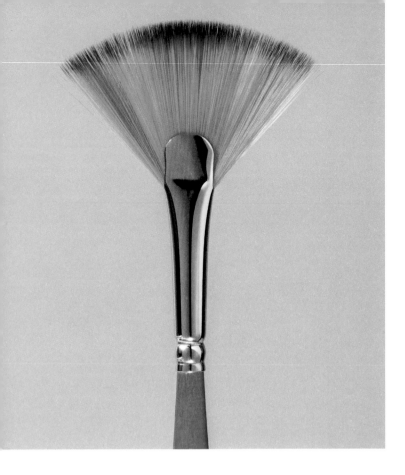

THANKS, I HATE IT
How to give feedback to art friends.

There is a heartbreaking scene in James Baldwin's 1962 novel, *Another Country*, in which Richard, a novelist and author of crime thrillers, accuses his wife of "despising" his creative work. "You seem to have so little respect for my success," he barks at her, before breaking down in tears. The presence of creative ambition within any relationship can be corrosive; the potential for judgment is always present. If that feedback turns negative, friendship—and even love—can sour.

When the stakes are so high, what should you do if you can't stand the artistic output of a close friend? Stay silent or speak up? It is first worth considering whether they really need to hear your honest thoughts. Will your feedback offer them a new way forward or will it simply drag them down? "Interpretation is the revenge of the intellect upon art," Susan Sontag argued, and the motivations behind that vengeance need to be carefully thought through.

Just as you wouldn't critique a friend's fashion choices or home decor, it is best to presume that their artwork is off-limits. But occasionally a friend will indicate that they crave candid appraisal amidst a sea of lickspittles too shy to speak up. Only if they have signified a desire for genuine reflection should you venture into this tricky territory.

Delivery and tone will be crucial. As W. Somerset Maugham wrote in *Of Human Bondage*, "People ask you for criticism, but they only want praise." Try mixing the bad with the good, and emphasize the elements that you have enjoyed before outlining the areas that you feel need more work.

Despite the confidence needed to put yourself out there as an artist, creatives can be a thin-skinned bunch. But even the greatest artists throughout history faced ridicule by strangers and friends alike. Take Swedish spiritualist painter Hilma Af Klint, who was so stung by her contemporaries' poor reception of her art that she left instructions in her will that it was not to be shown for 20 years after her death. The recent rediscovery of her work has led to exhibitions in museums around the world.

It just goes to show that our opinions and taste are often shaped by the social and political conditions in which we find ourselves. The dislike of a work of art often reflects more about the person who holds that view than about the artwork itself. An artist may not welcome the feedback of a friend, but they would do well to remember that the friend's opinion is ultimately entirely subjective, and to heed the words of British writer Will Self: "A creative life cannot be sustained by approval, any more than it can be destroyed by criticism."

WORDS
LOUISE BENSON
PHOTO
SERGIY BARCHUK

44

THE FRIENDSHIP PARADOX
On the probability of popularity.

Have you ever felt like your friends were more popular than you? Perhaps you're a little insecure about how many sexual partners you've had, or the number of connections you have on LinkedIn. The friendship paradox, a term coined by sociologist Scott L. Feld in 1991, would suggest these fears are not without foundation. It's down to sampling bias: You are more likely to be friends with someone who has more friends than you, simply because there is a greater chance that you will be friends with them. It's a quirk that's true of all social networks, whether they are in real life (most people's sexual partners tend to be more promiscuous than they are) or virtual (your followers on Instagram are more likely to have more followers than you).[1] The phenomenon has even been used to improve the detection of infectious diseases, allowing virologists to identify and monitor those people who are, on average, more popular, and therefore more likely to contract diseases than people in a random sample.

Although the friendship paradox works well on a theoretical level, it relies on a system of averages that don't, of course, describe everyone's experience. More recent studies have found that the accuracy of the friendship paradox depends on the social network in question. George Cantwell, a postdoctoral fellow at the Santa Fe Institute in New Mexico, found that while the paradox is true in friendship groups composed of people with varying degrees of popularity, this isn't all that common: Popular people are more likely to be friends with popular people and unpopular people with unpopular ones.

You might feel relieved that something as instinctive and genuine as friendship can't easily be explained by a sociological formula, but don't be. By taking these new assumptions into account, and by developing the concept of a "generalized friendship paradox," Cantwell and his team came up with an improved model: Your friends are not only more likely to be more popular than you, but, unfortunately, they will also be richer and better looking.

WORDS
GEORGE UPTON
PHOTO
RYAN DUFFIN

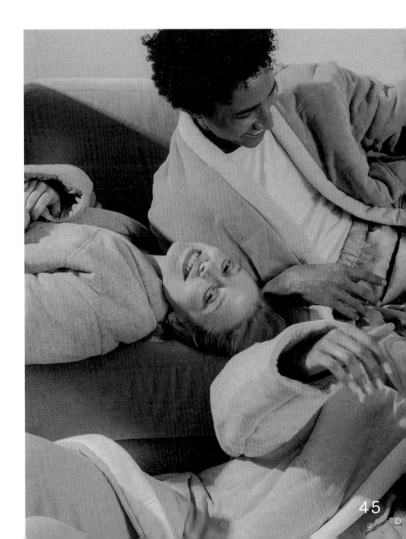

(1) The friendship paradox is more obvious in virtual spaces such as social media, where the size of a person's network is quickly visible. This may help explain why spending a lot of time online can lead to increased social anxiety.

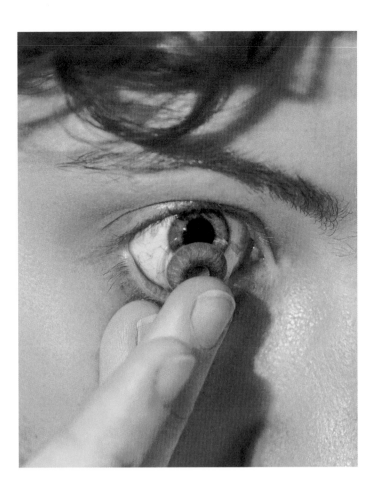

At the start of life, a name is a shot in the dark. Our official moniker says more about who our parents were than who we might become. Sometimes they make a lucky guess and the name sticks; sometimes it doesn't.

I dropped the letter "i" from my birthname, Tali, six years ago. Tal is a gender-neutral name, in sync with my nonbinary self. I haven't yet legally changed it and there are still people who use the old one. Often I remind them, sometimes I let it be. It's an ongoing journey.

Name changing is not necessarily a neat, linear process and each person has different considerations. You might already have chosen your new name—a variation on your old one, a long-held nickname, or a secret you've kept to yourself. Or you might feel overwhelmed by the possibilities; your old name isn't right, but what would be?

First, narrow down your options. Should your name reflect your new secular or religious way of life? Your gender? Your cultural heritage? Do you want a name that is noticed, or one that blends in with the crowd? A name that has some link to your old one—the same first letter, a similar meaning—or an entirely fresh start?

Next, brainstorm. You can look at lists online, filtered by gender or culture. You can trawl your family tree. Is there a biblical figure or contemporary celebrity who impresses you? You might take inspiration from a concept or attribute that resonates, from the natural world or from literature.

Try names out with close friends. Practice your new signature, sound out the syllables. Not everyone has a magical "click" moment, so take your time. A new name that feels unnatural at first could shift and grow on you. Some people go by their new name for months or years before deciding against it. But you can change your name more than once. This is a gift you're giving yourself; it's worth the effort.

WORDS
TAL JANNER-KLAUSNER
PHOTO
COREY OLSEN

HOW TO CHANGE A NAME
A short guide to finding what suits.

48 — 112

FEATURES
From Paris, Cape Town and LA.

48	Farida Khelfa	84	Home Tour: Vill'Alcina
58	Hot Desk	96	Essay: Holier Than Thou
68	Dr. Woo	100	Between Us
74	Preview: *Kinfolk Wilderness*	—	—

FÆRIDA KHELFA:

Words
DAPHNÉE DENIS

Photography
LUC BRAQUET

Styling
GIULIA QUERENGHI

FRANCE'S FASHION MUSE.

It was a split-second decision. She was out buying bread and bumped into a friend. Chatting and joking around outside her apartment building, they lost track of time. The next thing she knew, it was too late. Too late to get home unnoticed. Too late to avoid being told off by her parents. So she formed a plan, although you could hardly call it that, to leave everything behind—her family, her home and life as she'd known it in a housing project on the outskirts of Lyon.[1] Bread in hand, she hitchhiked her way to a railroad station, hopped on a train and hid away from conductors until the last stop. Farida Khelfa was 16. She had just made it to Paris, and was never to return.

Sitting across from her at her office in the eighth arrondissement of Paris, one of the most upscale neighborhoods in the city, it's hard to fathom what Khelfa went through back then. Since being a teenage runaway she's had a thousand lives: party girl, bouncer, model, muse, actor, head of the late couturier Azzedine Alaïa's design studio, couture director for Jean Paul Gaultier and documentary filmmaker. Yet she seems genuinely bemused when young people approach her to ask for a selfie, or tell her what she means to them as the first model of Algerian descent to make it in the industry, one whose features broke the mold of a white-centric fashion world. "I didn't realize it meant anything at all, I was just living life as a free woman, and let's just say I really went for it," Khelfa

"When I read what I lived through, I think it's crazy."

says, her laughter filling the room. She's traded the vintage looks that made her a 1980s style icon for designer clothes: today, a pair of baggy leather trousers and a dark blue knit sweater highlighting her bright red lips, her signature long dark curls now chopped in a bob cut. Hanging over her desk, a colorful painting by Congolese artist JP Mika, whose work she has championed as a collector of African art, provides a fitting caption to the scene. Its title is *Le goût de la réussite*, meaning "a taste for success."[2]

She tells me of how she spent time with her mother during the last months of her life and was able to ask her about her years in Algeria before the family moved to France—something they'd never discussed before. Understanding how her own story fit within that of previous generations prompted her to start writing it down, perhaps to make sense of it all. "When I read what I lived through, I think it's crazy, and if it were someone else writing about that life, I would be fascinated by it," she says. "But I never said to myself, *'Bloody hell, what a life you've had!'* Never."

(1) Khelfa grew up in cité des Minguettes, a housing project south of Lyon. After a series of riots erupted there during the 1980s, the area became emblematic of the vast social divides that exist within France.
(2) In a 2019 tour of Khelfa's Parisian townhouse, *Vogue Arabia* noted that her collection of contemporary African art, which includes pieces by Chéri Samba, George Lilanga and Moké, was "possibly the foremost in France."

Set Designer: Déborah Sadoun. Hair Stylist: Yumiko Hikage. Makeup: Ludivine François. Styling Assistant: Alice Heluin-Afchain

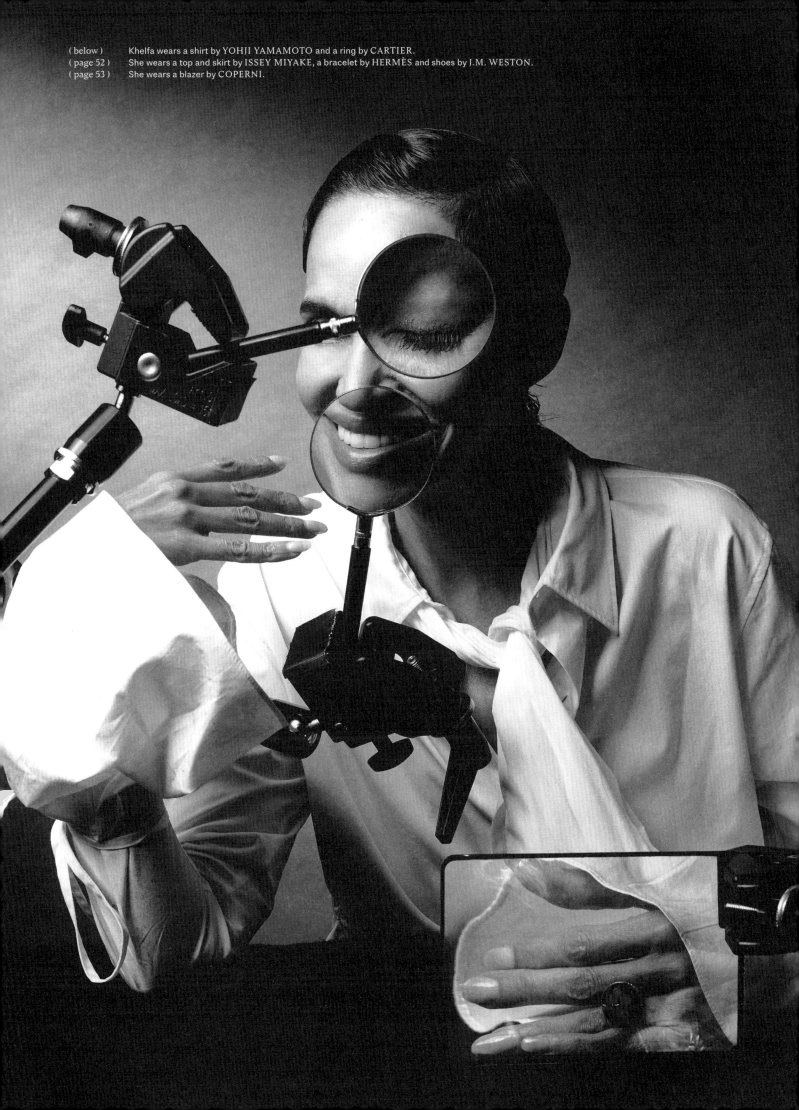

(below)   Khelfa wears a shirt by YOHJI YAMAMOTO and a ring by CARTIER.
(page 52)   She wears a top and skirt by ISSEY MIYAKE, a bracelet by HERMÈS and shoes by J.M. WESTON.
(page 53)   She wears a blazer by COPERNI.

An uncompromising longing for freedom seems to have guided much of Khelfa's trajectory. Born in 1960, she was one of 11 children of an Algerian immigrant couple who had fought for their country's independence from France alongside Algeria's National Liberation Front before moving the family to Lyon. Describing her parents, Khelfa says, "They were born colonized and remained colonized," meaning that, in her eyes, they never really overcame the humiliation of French rule.[3]

An avid reader from an early age, Khelfa explains that school was one of the places where she found freedom away from her strict household. She believes she would have gone on to study in university had she had "a normal family, whatever that means, if it even exists." Though she doesn't go into specifics, she describes her situation growing up as "painful," and says she decided to leave after her sisters moved out, leaving her, the youngest daughter, alone with her parents. Before the fateful day when an errand to the boulangerie became a one-way ticket to Paris, Khelfa had been carrying her Algerian passport everywhere for months. (France doesn't automatically grant citizenship to children born to foreign parents on French soil, so she would risk deportation if she was found without papers. She ultimately obtained French citizenship in her 30s.)

In Paris, Khelfa had planned on staying with one of her sisters, but quickly realized that wasn't an option. Things could have easily gone awry for a homeless teenager left to fend for herself in the French capital. Instead, that teenager met the coolest crowd in town: *"la bande du Palace."*

---

(3) After 132 years, the French colonization of Algeria ended following the 1954-62 French-Algerian war. In 2021, President Emmanuel Macron established a "memories and truth" commission to review what he had previously called "a crime against humanity" on France's part.

The Palace was Paris' response to New York's Studio 54. A former music hall, the flamboyant red and gold rococo venue reopened as a nightclub at the end of the 1970s and instantly brought together an unlikely bunch of partygoers—jet-setters, artists, intellectuals and absolute nobodies—all there to surrender to the power of disco music and dance the night away. Model, artist and provocateur Grace Jones performed on the club's opening night. Yves Saint Laurent and Loulou de la Falaise were regulars. So were philosopher Roland Barthes, Prince, David Bowie, Tina Turner, Jean Paul Gaultier and William Burroughs. It was in equal parts decadent and magnetic.

"Everyone went to The Palace, absolutely everyone," Khelfa recalls. "The most renowned intellectual, the biggest drug dealer, the kid from the projects, they all got in, that's what made it magical." Above all, it was an endless party. Almost as soon as she arrived in Paris, Khelfa met Edwige Belmore, a punk icon who would go on to become the bouncer at The Palace, and her roommate Paquita Paquin, a fashion journalist and avid club-goer. They introduced her to the city's party underworld, and the night creatures evolving in it, "super fun people with fantastic looks."[4]

Most evenings, Khelfa would go out dancing, unsure where she would sleep later. It didn't matter. She always found a place to crash. When a then-15-year-old Christian Louboutin invited her to sleep over at his mother's place, she ended up staying with them for months. He would sew her skirts with material from the Marché Saint-Pierre fabric district. The goal was to be stylish, always, even though she couldn't splurge on clothes. "I was young, everything seemed cool and easy," she recalls. "I never had any money but I never thought about the fact I had no money. It was freedom. We did what we wanted. We woke up when we wanted. It felt like a Godard film."[5]

It was at The Palace that Khelfa secured an introduction to an up-and-coming designer named Jean Paul Gaultier. One night, a woman who worked with him asked if she might be interested in modeling for one of his shows. Khelfa agreed to meet with him. "He was very shy, he didn't dare to look me in the eye," she says of their first encounter. "But I immediately saw that he liked me. He made me try on lots of clothes, and I felt comfortable in them; I knew how to walk even though I'd never done it before." Khelfa didn't take modeling too seriously. She was of two minds about it—honored to be picked out from the crowd, but also culturally uncomfortable with the idea of exposing herself. She would hide behind hanging rails to change clothes between turns on the runway, while the other models had no problem stripping in front of everyone. A self-professed "pain in the ass," Khelfa would only wear clothes she picked out herself and was surprised to find out other girls simply wore what they were told to. She worked with a handful of designers she liked. "The truth is, I was deeply insecure," she says, adding that

(4) From the late 1970s through to the early 1980s, The Palace was the focal point for the fashion world. Even the waiters wore Thierry Mugler–designed uniforms.

(5) Khelfa's husband, Henri Seydoux, is also a longtime friend of Christian Louboutin and the founder of the designer's eponymous luxury goods company.

(above)   Khelfa wears a coat by MM6 MAISON MARGIELA, a dress by DRIES VAN NOTEN and a necklace by CARTIER.
(page 56)   She wears a coat, sweater, collar and trousers by ANN DEMEULEMEESTER and shoes by J.M. WESTON.

finding herself backstage with the likes of Linda Evangelista, Cindy Crawford or Naomi Campbell was undeniably hard on the ego. "Then, I realized we all felt the same, we all checked each other out."

In a newscast from 1986, Gaultier introduces Khelfa, by then a close friend: "To me, she embodies beauty," he says as she clowns around, visibly uncomfortable to hear him complimenting her. "There's one beauty standard that's universally recognized, which is Greek beauty, a straight nose, etc., but I believe there's other forms of beauty, including Farida's, whose profile is fantastic. She has a beautiful nose, a beautiful mouth and a strong chin. For me, she's a star," he continues, as Khelfa grimaces and rolls her eyes, playing with her hair. She may not have fully grasped it then, but for a long time, hers was the only resolutely Arab-looking face to make it into high-end fashion magazines. "I believe she made many Maghrebis and Arabs feel represented in an industry that didn't see us," French-Tunisian stylist and fashion commentator Osama Chabbi tells me over email. "[Growing up], Farida's features felt very familiar to me—she's the women around me, my mother and aunts. It meant something to my younger self." When I tell her that supermodel Bella Hadid recently opened up about wishing she'd kept "the nose of her ancestors" instead of getting rhinoplasty, Khelfa sighs: "I'm so impressed by her, but maybe she wouldn't have had the same career."

" I never thought about the fact I had no money. It was freedom. We did what we wanted. It felt like a Godard film."

Some of Khelfa's most memorable images were snapped by her former partner, fashion photographer Jean-Paul Goude, whom she met at 22 while working as a bouncer at the nightclub Les Bains Douches. Goude took her picture for the cover of *Le Monde illustré*—a shot of her profile, her long, dark mane traversing the page in a seemingly endless wave.[6] The cover proclaimed her an icon of "le style beur," which roughly translates as "the Arab style" (the word "beur," which is now seen as derogatory, felt awkward almost as soon as it was invented, Khelfa says). Goude was the one to introduce Khelfa to perhaps her most meaningful collaborator, Tunisian designer Azzedine Alaïa. His many portraits of the duo capture their long-lasting friendship.

(6) Almost 30 years after their last photo shoot together, Jean-Paul Goude photographed Khelfa again for the October 2020 cover of *Vogue Arabia*. "She was fascinating, and she still is fascinating," Goude said at the time.

Even though she and Alaïa didn't really talk about it, their shared North African origins gave them an unspoken sense of kinship, says Khelfa. During fittings, he would play the music of Egyptian singer Umm Kulthum, and they would spend evenings watching Abdel Halim Hafez movies. She was more than a muse. It was with him that she decided to go after a role beyond modeling, as head of his design studio. He also gave her the confidence it would later take to pursue documentary filmmaking, she adds. "It was a great friendship, and a great loss too. It was really very hard to lose him."[7]

Now, as Khelfa has started writing her story, she realizes just "how insane" it all sounds. The golden age when she made her explosive entrance into the world of fashion may be long gone, but she doesn't feel nostalgic for the past. The most important thing—her friendships—have stood the test of time. "I'm loyal, and very grateful to the people who were there for me from the start," she says. Naomi Campbell and Elle Macpherson regularly pop up on her Instagram account. Gaultier and Louboutin are still among her closest friends, and became the subjects of two of her documentaries, when she decided she would be more comfortable behind the camera than in front of it. "I'd been offered a TV presenter job, and I didn't feel up to the task," she says of getting her first documentary commission. "But the producer who had approached me was also working on a profile of Jean Paul Gaultier, so I told him: 'That, I can do, I know him well and I've never seen something that reflects who he really is.' On the first day of the shoot, I thought, *Am I crazy?* But actually, it went well."

Through it all, Khelfa has remained a fixture at fashion shows around the world. *Vanity Fair France* named her among the 30 most stylish celebrities of 2022 and, in October of the same year, she closed Naomi Campbell's Fashion for Relief EMERGE runway show in Doha, Qatar, alongside Campbell and Janet Jackson. Still, her craft as a filmmaker is what motivates her now: In 2017, she left her role as muse of the Schiaparelli fashion house to focus on "personal artistic projects" and has made storytelling her main focus since then.

In her latest film, *From the Other Side of the Veil*, Khelfa celebrates Muslim women in the Middle East, and challenges narratives reducing those wearing head coverings as victims with no agency or ambition—a particularly thorny issue in France, where teenagers can't attend school wearing a hijab. Forcing women to put on—or, indeed, remove—any items of clothing is "so backward," she tells me: "And they believe these girls will remove their headscarves just because they are told to…. It's never going to happen."[8] She gives an eye roll and, for a quick moment, I think of the rebellious teenager who left home to live life by her own set of rules. She would know. Freedom has always been her guiding force.

---

(7)   Alaïa died in Paris in 2017, at the age of 82. Khelfa traveled to the village of Sidi Bou Said, Tunisia, for his funeral.
(8)   "Women in the Middle East are just like other women around the world, we're all fighting for our rights," Khelfa told *AnOther* magazine on release of the film. "Seeing them as victims is a colonial point of view."

" I'm loyal, and very
grateful to the people
who were there for me
from the start."

(top) Khelfa wears a vest by MATERIEL and a bracelet by CARTIER.
(bottom) She wears a bodysuit by ALAÏA, trousers and hat by ANN
DEMEULEMEESTER and jewelry by HERMÈS.

The many faces of
a multifunctional
workstation.

59   HOT DESK

Photography
CECILIE JEGSEN
Styling
DENIS BJERREGAARD

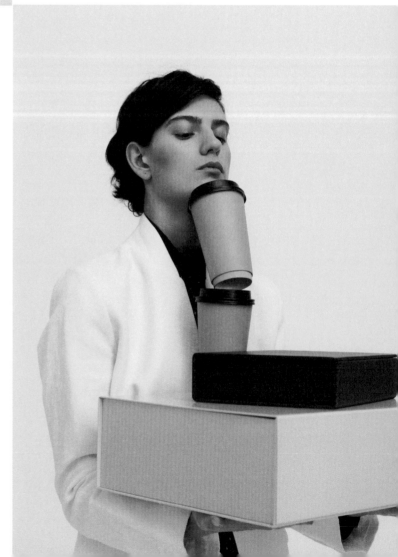

(previous)   Aida wears a blazer by AERON, a shirt from the stylist's archive, a tie by ZEGNA, trousers by AÉRÉ and shoes by NODALETO.
(top left)   She wears a blazer by AERON, a shirt from the stylist's archive and a tie by ZEGNA.
(bottom left)   She wears a blazer by MARK KENLY DOMINO TAN and a shirt and tie from the stylist's archive.
(below)   She wears a dress and cardigan by BIRROT, a shirt by DRIES VAN NOTEN and earrings by TIFFANY & CO.

(below)　　Aida wears a vest by AÉRÉ, a dress and trousers by BIRROT, shoes by NODALETO and a bag by AESTHER EKME.
(opposite)　　She wears trousers by AÉRÉ and shoes by NODALETO.

(above)   Aida wears a coat by HERMÈS.
(top right)   She wears a vest by AÉRÉ and a shirt by DRIES VAN NOTEN.
(bottom right)   She wears a sweater, shirt and skirt by Birrot, earrings by TIFFANY & CO. and shoes by NODALETO.

Q&A:
CASSANDRA BRADFIELD
Words by Harriet Fitch Little

*Four questions for the
designer commissioned to create the multifunctional desk featured in this story.*

HFL: How did you think about the challenge of creating a multifunctional object for this collaboration?

CB: I wanted to make an object that had a balance of mass and negative space, like a series of construction planes coming together. From there it was: *How can I make these planes be in line with the heights of the table, stool, shelf and desk?*

HFL: Do you often design with lots of different uses in mind?

CB: When you create something rather simple it can end up feeling more flexible. This is especially true in interior design. One of the most satisfying parts of designing both furniture and spaces is seeing all the ways the user breaks the obvious initial design intention.

HFL: How do you think about the relationship between form and function?

CB: Functionality is generally what separates design from art. As a designer, I feel both boxes need to be checked.

HFL: What else are you working on?

CB: At the moment I'm working on a few furniture projects with my colleague, Sofia Olsson, at our newly founded collaborative venture, Asca Studio. We're mounting a seven-meter-high chandelier at the new Stockholm Soho House this week. At Studio Cassandra Bradfield, I'm working on some bespoke residential interiors.

Hair & Makeup: Malene Kirkegaard. Model: Aida at Unique Models.

(below)   Aida wears a vest by AÉRÉ, a shirt by DRIES VAN NOTEN and a tie from the stylist's archive.
(opposite)   She wears a sweater, shirt and skirt by BIRROT, earrings by TIFFANY & CO. and a bag by AESTHER EKME.

DR. WOO:

Photography
JUSTIN CHUNG

Words
MARIANNE ELOISE

MEET THE TATTOO ARTIST WHO'S INKED LA.

The making of a celebrity tattoo artist is difficult to trace. They are not always more talented or visionary than their peers, or more aggressive in their pursuit of the spotlight. The shift to fame can happen seemingly overnight: One day they are toiling away in someone else's studio, the next day musicians and actors are lining up to be inked by them. So it was for DR. WOO.

Photo Assistant: Julien Sage

Now in his 40s, the LA-based artist's work first exploded in popularity in 2016, and today his celebrity clients include Frank Ocean, Justin and Hailey Bieber, Kid Cudi, Miley Cyrus and Zoë Kravitz.

Some aspects of Woo's lore are exaggerated: The story that he called himself Dr. Woo to please an overbearing parent is something he let run because it's "funny." (In reality, he says, his parents are just happy that he's given them two grandchildren.) He doesn't really have a two-year waiting list; it would be suffocating to book that far ahead. He doesn't have much of an ego, either. Introducing himself as Brian on the phone, he is clear, humble and in love with his practice. He talks about his compositions in exacting detail, like he's conducting an orchestra.

Once you know what you're looking for, Woo's work—and its imitators—are recognizable anywhere: small, intricate, single-needle designs in gray tones. Taking cues from Los Angeles culture, his signature pieces include palm trees, animals and geometric patterns. This style took a while to develop. He started getting tattooed at 11 with his friends (sewing needles and Indian ink) and at 14 got his first real tattoo at a studio off Melrose Avenue. "I remember it was Thanksgiving because the artist was on the phone asking where to get a turkey last minute. He told me, 'If your parents ask you where you got this tattoo, you gotta tell them you went to Mexico,'" says Woo. "He knew I was young, but he didn't care enough not to do it." The piece, a small dragon on his ankle, moved as he grew and is now somewhere around the middle of his calf.

As an 18-year-old at the turn of the millennium, he started to collect tattoos by well-regarded artists. Among them was Mark Mahoney, the proprietor of Shamrock Social Club in Hollywood, who was a "god" to him and his friends. But Woo had no intention of becoming a tattoo artist himself. He tried college, then worked as an assistant buyer for a skate shop. He was also running his own clothing brand, but it never went very far: "I got bogged down, and it was hard to get backers and people interested." During that time, he was hanging out at Mahoney's shop, getting a lot of tattoos and competing with his friends to be the most covered.

When Woo was in his early 20s, Mahoney asked if he had ever considered becoming a tattoo artist. Woo felt that he was the antithesis of the guys he was getting tattooed by: A first-generation immigrant born to Taiwanese parents, he looked and felt different from the men in the industry. "I was intimidated because everyone in the shop looked like they were born a tattoo artist, and I wasn't. I was born into a very conservative Asian family. It was scary!" But it felt right. The story goes that he quit his job the next day. (Actually, he says now, there's some myth in there: He did both jobs for a week or two before going "all in.")

For a few years, Woo apprenticed without even touching a machine. He was the first to arrive at the shop and the last to leave, helping to set up for the day, clean equipment and take care of any administrative work that needed doing. "I wanted to be completely organic and do it the right way," he says. When he finally got behind a machine, he was learning from Mahoney, who he describes as one of the first "champions" of single-needle tattooing. "I learned my technique and style from Mark. He was doing it in a very old-school way in terms of the subject matter and the style, but he made it his own."

At the time, most well-known tattoo artists were pushing designs that were big and bold: dragons, tribal tattoos, skulls, naked women, maybe a little blood here and there. But tastes were changing and evolving technology made delicate, hyper-detailed tattoos possible. Woo developed his own spin on Mahoney's style, something he credits in part to the input of his early clients. "A lot of them were artists and creatives, so the ideas started getting really cool. They found the strength and density in minimalism where the fewer lines there were, the more impact it held." This put him onto the idea of "telling small, detailed stories that you could hide and that could be a little bit anonymous on the skin."

There is uncertainty in Woo's voice when he discusses what happened next. It was difficult, he says, when he became more successful than his peers and mentors. While still at Shamrock, he had started to share his work on Instagram: "It got crazy. There was a lot of attention and demand, but it was tough because I was the lowest on the totem pole in the shop," Woo says. He felt like the success was undeserved compared to his colleagues who had been toiling away for years. It made for complicated workplace politics. "I had to respect my fellow artists and my boss while growing. I felt shame about the success because I didn't want to feel like I was overstepping my boundaries or competing with these other guys."

He attributes his success not to being better, but to his delicate style becoming popular. In fact, when he became so overbooked that he couldn't see everyone, his colleagues adopted it. "I was bringing a lot of business into the shop, but it was bittersweet. It was good for the shop but bad for my relationships." Looking back, he feels some sadness over those complex workplace dynamics, but he mostly feels proud. "Mark created this shop where all these fine line tattoos were coming from. It took me a long time to understand that it's not *not* being humble to recognize your position and your work."

Woo now works out of a private studio, which adds to the mystique—you only find out the location when you secure a coveted booking. But what remains the same is that he's in LA, the city he grew up in and the only one he can imagine living in. "This is all I've ever known. . . . There's something special about this city, we're different cultures living on top of each other. There's no racial divide." He sees it, rather optimistically, as

"The fewer lines there were, the more impact it held."

a center for opportunity, a place where you can show up with two bucks and figure it out. As well as tattooing, Woo has launched a skincare line (with a focus on products that will be gentle to freshly inked skin), the coffee table book *Everything is Permanent* and collaborations with brands including Sacai, Roger Dubuis and Jean Paul Gaultier.

No matter who the artist is—and how hyped they are—tattooing is simple. It's about driving ink into skin. It's about making a permanent decision that you may regret, but if you have the right relationship with the right artist, you might not. Rapport can outlive a session; part of what Woo's clients are paying for is membership in his club. So, what of that mythical two-year waitlist? Woo shuts it down. "If you're that booked out, you are lucky to be successful in business, but it's almost like handcuffs," he says. Woo has a flexible schedule wherein if he's home and working, his assistant gets people in. Even after almost a decade of success, he is superstitious about saying his books are full: "It's like saying 'Bloody Mary' in the mirror. If I vocalize it, I'm going to curse it. I feel blessed to even be booked at all."

(opposite)   In 2021, Woo collaborated with Swiss watchmaker Roger Dubuis to create a new timepiece.

Preview:

THE ARDENNES

Photography
MARTIN PAUER

In an excerpt from our latest book,
Kinfolk Wilderness, ANNICK WEBER takes a horseback
ride through Belgium's sylvan splendor.

While riding a horse, there sometimes comes a point when you feel both grounded and outside of yourself, connected both with your surroundings and with another living being. The Belgian Ardennes offers an ideal setting for anyone hoping to achieve this sensation. Hacking through thick woods and across trickling streams on horseback, riders get a taste of the freedom that comes from time spent with nature.

Located halfway between Brussels and Luxembourg City in Belgium's southeastern corner, the Belgian Ardennes is a land of charming beauty. Cows graze in verdant pastures, and the picture-perfect ruins of medieval castles rest atop steep river valleys. Deep in the heart of the region lies the Grande Forêt de Saint-Hubert, a sparsely populated 247,000-acre forest teeming with game and thousands of miles of marked hiking, mountain biking and horse-riding trails. "You can go for hours without crossing a single village or paved road, and yet the landscape is so varied that it will never get boring," says trek leader Dirk de Ridder. "People love exploring the region on foot or by bike, but it's even better in the saddle. It gives you more time to soak up the natural beauty."

De Ridder was instrumental in developing the Chevauchée Forestière, a 104-mile looped trail ride through the Grande Forêt de Saint-Hubert. Designed for riders of all levels whether alone on their own steed or accompanied by de Ridder and one of his four well trained Rocky Mountain horses—the trek takes about five days to complete, but de Ridder arranges shorter routes for those with less time. While camping is possible in the forest's dedicated campgrounds (wild camping is illegal), the trail's organizers have teamed up with hotels and bed-and-breakfasts in local villages where both humans and animals can find shelter—a comfortable bed for the former, a lush paddock for the latter. It makes for a less cumbersome trek, requiring only the bare minimum of equipment: weather-appropriate clothing and snacks; brushes and hoof picks are provided by the guide. There's nothing more liberating than reducing your belongings to what fits into two saddlebags.

(opposite)   The sturdy front legs of an Ardennais horse, one of the oldest
European breeds. In this region of the Ardennes, the horses are still
deployed for farm work and heavy drafting, such as logging.

(left)
The trail's terrain may be challenging at times, but de Ridder works with Rocky Mountain horses, a breed that was originally developed for farms in the Appalachian foothills and that is said to be both calm and courageous.

(opposite) Château de Mirwart is a boutique hotel that traces its roots back to the eighth century. The castle is located in the picturesque village of Mirwart, which is at the heart of the Saint-Hubert forest.

For seasoned equestrians, the Chevauchée Forestière boasts stretches of open fields to gallop through, but the real reward lies in a slower, fit-for-all-levels pace of travel. Because of the area's rugged topography, the horses often can't travel faster than a gentle walk up and down narrow forest tracks. These might lead you to lookout points offering panoramic views of the Semois River snaking below, to craggy hilltops where your hair blows in the wind or to shallow waters and streams. The trek is a multisensory experience: Your body fills with endorphins, the greenery takes on a brilliant hue in the dappled sunlight and the breeze carries the scent of the surrounding pine trees. The terrain might be challenging at times, but riding through a sea of ferns or across soft blankets of moss to the sound of birdsong overhead is a panacea for body and soul.

In this sparsely populated region, it's not uncommon to spot wildlife along the way. More often than not, just after sunrise, herds of deer and wild boar can be seen running through the woodland; a reason to set off early. Another familiar sight along the Chevauchée Forestière is the Ardennais draft horse, a breed with a particularly bulky build and thick legs, which is still used for logging on forest grounds inaccessible by machinery.

(opposite) Plan a detour to pass through Redu, a picturesque village whose cobbled streets are lined with dozens of bookshops. There's a small but well curated art museum, Mudia, which displays over 300 works spanning seven centuries.

The Grande Forêt de Saint-Hubert is also a popular hunting ground and, come mid-autumn, parts of it close for hunting season. On your ride, you will come across the odd turreted château, or castle, built in the 19th century as hunting lodges by the Belgian bourgeoisie. The castle grounds, some of which are open for riders, are often dotted with fishing ponds where you can stop for a scenic picnic and your horse can graze and have a drink.

Though every season in the Ardennes has its draw, de Ridder recommends visiting on either side of the summer months, when nature is at its most vibrant. In late spring, the riverbeds are flanked by wildflower meadows, while in early fall the rolling hills are awash with golden colors. "Sometimes I send friends photos of the scenery I pass on my rides and they ask me which faraway country I'm in, but I prefer not to tell them," he says with a smile. Indeed, the Belgian Ardennes—unspoiled and largely unvisited by international travelers—is a secret worth keeping.

This story is an exclusive excerpt from our forthcoming book, *Kinfolk Wilderness*. Pre-order at Kinfolk.com now, or shop in stores worldwide from April 11.

Photography
MARINA DENISOVA

HOME TOUR:

Words
AGNISH RAY

VILL'ALCINA

For nearly 50 years, architect SERGIO FERNANDEZ has found political purpose and refuge at his vacation home.

Drive an hour north from Porto and the landscape becomes hilly. As I head toward the town of Caminha, the road winds into the valleys, while waves crash onto the shores of the vast ocean stretching out to the left. We're by Portugal's border with the Spanish region of Galicia, whose Santa Tecla mountain rises tall across the bay.

When the architect Sergio Fernandez acquired a patch of land here, on a hillside overlooking the mouth of the Minho river, there were no homes nearby. It was the early 1970s, and he built two identical houses side by side, one for himself and another for the friend with whom he had purchased the plot. "I wanted it to be similar to the land," explains Fernandez, who has driven me from Porto to his mountain retreat. At 85, he is nimble of form, sharp of mind and energetic of spirit. He is also as clear as ever on the building principles that have driven his six-decade practice: "Made for people. No high technics. A sense of being real."

The house reveals itself from the road, its red cement roof peeking out from among the foliage above. The air is fragrant with eucalyptus and pine. Creepers climb up the concrete and granite structure and a blue and white sign by the entrance announces the name of the abode: Vill'Alcina. A single sloping roof unifies the whole construction, its angle mimicking the incline of the hill.

Architecture students are often brought to this rural refuge—it is celebrated as an example of how a home's design can be determined by its natural environments—but its owner never imagined his personal venture would become such a case study. Instead, this creation was guided by modesty, comfort and a carefree spirit that delights in quirky touches, whether in composition or decoration. "The important thing is the quality of the space," Fernandez says. "I don't mind if things seem slightly careless—I wanted the house to have a spirit."

On descending the steps into the house, the first thing I notice is how few hard separations there are at Vill'Alcina. "The idea was to allow everyone to share it all the time," the architect explains. Cooking, dining and lounge areas are spread across two levels, but the space is open and free, designed around a chimney that acts as its focal point. The bedrooms' layout is similarly relaxed, with a dormitory-like feeling that children adore. Wooden walls and floors in the sleeping areas keep the temperature down in summer.

"No clients want this kind of solution," says Fernandez, who delighted at having free rein over the spatial arrangement. "This isn't a house to live ¡in every day¡—it's for holidays and free time. So I thought it would be more interesting to have common, continuous space." For nearly 50 years now he's spent weekends and vacations here, sharing the space with loved ones who come to stay. He opens red wooden shutters to reveal the

(below) Vill'Alcina combines classic mid-century furniture with more eclectic designs, such as the vintage dumbwaiter pictured by the window.
(opposite) Born in 1937, Fernandez grew up under the autocratic Estado Novo government. The architecture encouraged by the regime was grand concrete structures with classical ornamentation, a world away from the naturalism that Fernandez and his contemporaries pursued.

property's dramatic Atlantic view, which is dappled by the wild trees—oak, cork, bay, holly—that populate the grounds.

Fernandez's humility conceals the magnitude of his experience. Once a student of Fernando Távora and professor to Eduardo Souto de Moura, both Pritzker Prize winners from Porto, he is among the generation of architects who witnessed the formation of a new architectural identity in Portugal amid radical political change.

Fernandez's youth was spent in fear of the authoritarian Estado Novo's political police. "It was impossible to have a conversation like this in a café," he says. "We were limited—but this gave us strength and imagination."

Back then, practices like art and architecture became synonymous with the resistance. While the country's dictator, António de Oliveira Salazar, fantasized about the awesome and intimidating architectural visions of fascist Germany and Italy, the modern reality of Portugal proved totally opposite, characterized by comfort, functionality and a sense of place. "We were all engaged in the revolution," Fernandez explains. "Being a good professional meant being against the regime." After 48 years, Salazar's rule was overthrown on April 25, 1974—incidentally, Fernandez's birthday. Vill'Alcina was completed that same year: the perfect retreat for his first summer holidays in the newly liberated Portugal that he had longed for.

For the nation's architects, the change opened new channels for influences, from Le Corbusier to Alvar Aalto. It also inspired new ways of thinking about buildings—modern, but respectful of local tradition. "We gave much more value to our natural things, a notion of scale, the right use of local materials,"

says Fernandez. "We discovered the country that we knew existed but couldn't feel."

His worldly interests have been intrinsic to his development as a practitioner. He's traveled extensively with Fernando Távora and Álvaro Siza (the latter is considered by many to be Portugal's greatest living architect and has been Fernandez's friend since his teenage years), devouring the architec-

Wooden walls help to naturally regulate the temperature of the house. Wood has low thermal conductivity, meaning it both gains and loses heat slowly.

tural delights of places like Greece, Egypt and Brazil. In the mid-1960s he even traveled to Brasilia with its architect, Oscar Niemeyer, when the city was just four or five years old. The two drove all the way from Rio de Janeiro because Niemeyer hated flying.

Fernandez had more reason than most to be interested in the meeting points of different cultures. The architect's mother

(named Alcina; she is the home's namesake) was from Porto, while his father was from Barcelona, so he grew up speaking a mix of Portuguese, Catalan and Spanish. The consumption of food and culture at home was similarly multicultural, equipping him with a thirst for travel. The eclectic decor at Vill'Alcina reflects this adventurous spirit, with pieces from India, Brazil, Morocco, Macao, Cuba and beyond. A blue ceramic Hand of Fatima amulet, a figurine traditional of Bengali craft and several North African rugs sit alongside wooden birds, bowls of pine cones, bouquets of dried flowers and an old corn mill.

Today, Fernandez enjoys his leisure time but hasn't abandoned his career. He continues work with his studio, Atelier 15, whose projects range from private residences to heritage restorations across the country, from the Santa Clara church in Coimbra to ancient gems in the Roman town of Idanha-a-Velha. They recently finished work on the Batalha theater in Porto, an art deco building from 1947, where they reinstated communist symbols on the theater's facade that were removed during Salazar's dictatorship. They also uncovered murals that had been painted over by authorities.

These are powerful acts for Fernandez and his peers, who have spent recent decades reevaluating Portugal's architectural and political legacy. Vill'Alcina may be one of his more humble, experimental projects but it's marked by history, both personal and public. The open, free-flowing layout of the rustic getaway also embodies the spirit of freedom and divergence from established structures that energized his radical generation. "The house was conceived exactly before the revolution," he explains. "It was linked with our desire for liberty."

(opposite)   Vill'Alcina looks down over the Minho river, an estuary that separates Portugal from Spain.

"We were all engaged in the revolution. Being a good professional meant being against the regime."

On the state of
celebrity affairs.

ESSAY:
HOLIER THAN THOU

Words
STEPHANIE
D'ARC TAYLOR

In the pantheon of fun days to be online, leaked celebrity sexts rank right up there. A famous man—it's almost always a man—is brought low in the face of a beautiful stranger's mirror selfie, reduced to lusty babbling over text.

Titans of their fields, from Tiger Woods to Jeff Bezos to Salman Rushdie, have been caught—and mocked for—sending messages ranging from flirty to filthy.[1] But the most recent rash of leaks exist in a media ecosystem that seems designed to stoke discord and widespread condemnation over even relatively minor transgressions. A future historian poring over the online archives of fall 2022 might conclude that American society in the 21st century was more prurient than it had been in the one prior. In September 2022, Adam Levine, a California pop star and judge of a televised singing competition,

model Emily Ratajkowski weighed in. "If you're the one in the relationship, you're the one who's obligated to be loyal." The colleagues with whom Fulmer made his video content, the other "Try Guys," posted a scolding, scandalized video and edited Fulmer out of content they had already shot.

The gleeful or righteous reactions to such revelations are understandable impulses. It's a "stars, they're just like us" moment. What's more, according to media scholar Claire Sisco King, scandalized (and faux-scandalized) reactions to famous men cheating is a tale as old as celebrity itself. "When tabloid magazines were first created in the 1950s [they focused on] allegations of sex scandals of famous people, from extramarital affairs to allegations of same-sex relationships," says King, who is chair of the cinema and media arts program at Vanderbilt University. What *is* new, she

> " That leads to a much more complicated question: Is having an affair the same thing as being a misogynist?"

was caught sending carnally appreciative direct messages (DMs) to attractive young women other than his pregnant wife. If the screenshots are to be believed, "I may need to see the booty" was one of the sweet nothings he tapped out on his smartphone before hitting send. Days later, the online personality Ned Fulmer, known for being one of *Buzzfeed*'s "Try Guys" and for his gushy social media posts about his wife and family, admitted to an extramarital affair with an employee. With these two revelations, the internet meme machine went into overdrive. "It's truly unreal how fucking hot you are"—Levine's reaction to a picture of a model in a bikini—was superimposed over images as varied as Danny DeVito wearing a dress and the *Star Wars* character Jar Jar Binks.[2]

But the hilarity was tempered with reproach, aimed squarely at Levine. "I don't understand why we continue to blame women for men's mistakes,"

says, are responses to celebrity sex scandals in the age of "digital intermediation"—which those of us outside the academy might refer to as the age of TikTok.

Stars are closer to us than ever. Gone are the days when you'd find out what color was in vogue for the season by standing for hours at the castle walls hoping for a glimpse of the king's raiment, or when only an exclusive magazine interview would shed light on an actor's diet regimen. Now, with smartphones and reality television, celebrities are—and are expected to be—constantly

(1)   Leaked Facebook messages showed Rushdie telling the socialite and editor Devorah Rose that she looked "gorgeous and hottt!" It was not an inappropriate message (the two had been dating) but garnered attention because it was so out of step with the venerated author's public persona.

(2)   Levine's messages went viral partly because people found them funny. As Don Caldwell, editor in chief of *Know Your Meme*, told *Wired*: "It's like a teenage boy wrote them, which makes them super memeable."

accessible, warts and all. "What social media has done," says King, "is exaggerate these expectations between famous people and their fans. When celebrities share with us their personal struggles, it amplifies the sense among audience members that they have an intimate relationship."[3] On top of that, social media famously confers confidence in its users to say things online they might not say to someone face-to-face. People feel that speaking their most extreme opinions online is their right.

But this isn't just the age of TikTok. In the US, where the majority of this discourse is taking place, it's also the age of a great reckoning of gender-based violence, discrimination and exploitation. There is a movement of "bottom-up shaming as a mechanism for holding powerful figures accountable," says Henry Jenkins, a media scholar at the University of Southern California.

" When celebrities share their personal struggles, it amplifies the sense among audience members that they have an intimate relationship."

According to Jessica Calvanico, a feminist scholar at Rutgers University, canceling a pop personality for sending a sexy DM—frankly no more or less cringey than any other sexy DM seen out of context—may feel like justice in a world where "actual consequences for the people who really deserve them are not manifesting." But "people wrongly equate those things," Calvanico argues. Editing a co-star out of your TikTok videos because he had a consensual relationship with someone other than his wife doesn't do a thing to combat the very real misogyny running rampant throughout the highest echelons of our society.[4] "It's a performative way of combating misogyny. To me that leads to a much more complicated question: Is having an affair the same thing as

(3)   These are known as parasocial relationships. A term first coined in the 1950s, it has become increasingly common to describe the relationship fans have with celebrities, particularly those who use social media to share their lives online.

(4)   As well as editing Fulmer out of videos, the Try Guys also canned some projects they had already been working on because Fulmer featured in them. Many online commentators saw this as a bizarre overreaction.

being a misogynist? While some forms of woman-izing are a form of misogyny, I don't think those are necessarily the same thing," Calvanico says.

"We're witnessing a shift in how we think about gender and sexuality," she continues. "That's evidenced by #MeToo, and also by a newfound acceptance of different forms of gender identi-ties and sexual configurations and lifestyles. As a feminist, that's exciting to me." The outrage and mockery of Levine and Fulmer are part of a pro-cess of "deciding what's okay and what's not okay" for modern ideas of sexuality and relationships. "I think these are growing pains," she says. Perhaps we've gone too far in some cases—interpreting garden-variety relationship misbehavior as abus-es of power. Distracting someone to the point of slack-jawed unintelligibility is arguably the very aim of sexting in the first place.

But making a mockery of celebrities' minor transgressions may have some larger value, says Calvanico. Part of what lets politicians, film pro-ducers and other celebrities get away with sex-ual harassment or violence is the power soci-ety grants them due to their elevated status. We buy into celebrities' "performance of an authen-tic self," as Calvanico puts it, which isn't actually very authentic at all. That's why it's newsworthy when celebrities do anything remotely relatable, whether that's embarrassing themselves in a DM or picking up a coffee from Dunkin' Donuts.[5]

"I think tearing down and dismantling the fa-cade [of celebrity] is always a worthwhile endeav-or," says Calvanico. "In these relatively harmless examples, particularly the Levine one—which is not the same as a female celebrity being doxed or her nudes being leaked—this minimal jesting is interesting because it helps to chip away at the pedestal that celebrity culture has assumed in this moment." By eroding the barriers that have tra-ditionally protected celebrities from being held to normal standards, perhaps we'll begin to see them—and ourselves—more clearly.

(5)   One of the media's favorite examples of a celebrity being "just like us" is Ben Affleck and his obsession with Dunkin' Donuts. Affleck has no financial partnership with the brand, but is often described as its biggest marketing tool due to his sheer devotion to their iced coffees and snacks. During the pandemic, paparazzi photographers would frequently wait outside his home to snap him picking up doorstep deliveries from Dunkin'.

The world looks
brighter among
old friends.

101   BETWEEN US

Photography
MICHAEL
OLIVER LOVE
Styling
MANDY NASH

(previous and left)   All models wear looks from the stylist's archive.
(below)   Jude wears a kimono by DIANA CILLIERS and trousers by LUKHANYO MDINGI.
Robyn wears a kimono by VIVIERS and leggings from the stylist's archive.

Hair: Inga Hewett. Makeup: Chloe Hicks. Photo Assistant: Tiano Xavier. Production Manager: Aaron Sacks

(below)   Liam and Jude wear looks by AKJP STUDIO.
(opposite)   Liam, Robyn and Claudia wear looks by LUKHANYO MDINGI.

(above)　　　　Lehlohonolo, Claudia, Robyn, Candace and Liam wear looks from the stylist's archive.
(top right)　　Liam and Jude wear looks by LUKHANYO MDINGI.
(bottom right)　All models wear items from the stylist's archive.

(opposite)   Lehlohonolo and Claudia wear looks by SELFI.
(below)   All models wear looks by SLEEPER from AKJP STUDIO.

(opposite)   All models wear looks by SLEEPER from AKJP STUDIO.
(below)   Lehlohonolo and Claudia wear looks by LUKHANYO MDINGI.
(overleaf)   All models wear items from the stylist's archive.

(opposite)   All models wear looks by SLEEPER from AKJP STUDIO.
(below)   Lehlohonolo and Claudia wear looks by LUKHANYO MDINGI.
(overleaf)   All models wear items from the stylist's archive.

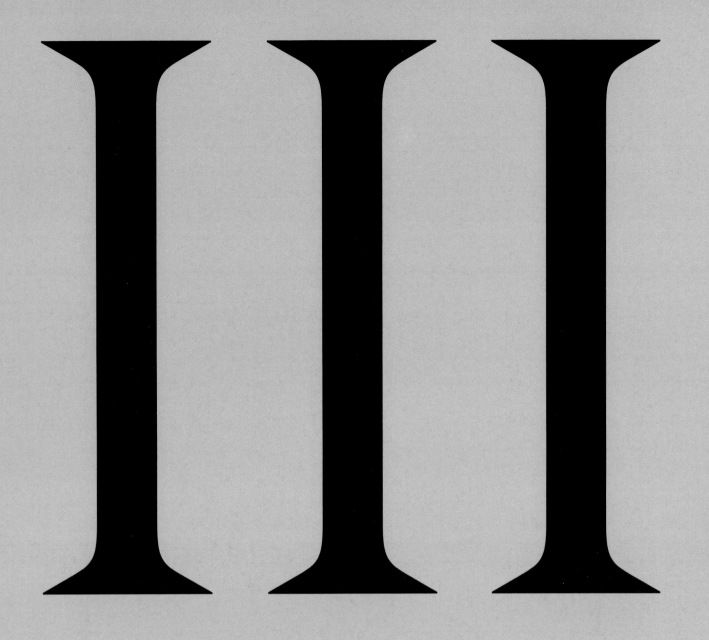

III

114 — 176

WELL-BEING
Self-acceptance, salaries and duvet days.

Part I: The Body
116   Dancing with Alice Sheppard
126   Sobriety with Julia Bainbridge
134   Essay: Too Much of a Good Thing
—   —

Part II: The Mind
140   Therapy with Walt Odets
150   Chani Nicholas and Sonya Passi
158   Wild Nights and Duvet Days
168   A Picture of Health

Body

DANCING
with

Words
LOUISE BRUTON

ALICE SHEPPARD

On dance as a channel to commune with
the body — even when it hurts.

Photography
TED BELTON

Alice Sheppard fell into dance on a dare. Spurred on by a disabled dancer she met at a conference, the former English and comparative literature lecturer took her first lesson in 2004. Studying ballet, modern dance and wheelchair technique under the disability activist Kitty Lunn of Infinity Dance Theater, she became a touring member of the AXIS Dance Company within three years. By 2012, Sheppard was performing as an independent artist with Ballet Cymru, GDance and Full Radius Dance, among others, but soon she would take on a challenge of her own. Having founded the disability arts ensemble Kinetic Light in 2016, Sheppard's vision as artistic director is to create work that connects with and draws from disability culture. Splitting her time between New York and San Francisco, two contrasting cities she considers home, the British choreographer and dancer says she goes "where the work is."

As two wheelchair users, Sheppard and I share a vantage point, and this familiarity breeds a mutual fondness. In our conversation around artistic expression and care, we laugh, we scrutinize and we dig deep. Sheppard expertly navigates the subtext of anything that's asked of her as a disabled artist—indeed, of anything that's asked of disabled people, such as when I ask how dance contributes to her well-being. "The question that people are actually wanting to know when they ask that question is: How does dance make my body better with regard to disability?" This isn't a question she's interested in answering.

Although she rolls her eyes at wellness culture as commodified by celebrities, Sheppard is keen to talk about the ways in which the well-being of disabled people depends on our environment, even if it's one that we have to create for ourselves.

LOUISE BRUTON: Can you remember the first time you connected with dance?

ALICE SHEPPARD: Shortly—but not immediately—after becoming disabled, I made the annual pilgrimage with the same group of friends to *The Nutcracker*. Soon after the beginning of act two, I just lost it. Like nothing on earth—tears just coming and coming. It was all very awkward. I think people likely thought of it as a disability thing, as me crying because I could not do what I was seeing. I didn't experience it that way. Or, at least, I didn't actively experience it that way. To this day, I'm not sure what set me off.

LB: What is your relationship with wellness culture?

AS: I want to separate what I think contemporary wellness culture is from the disability world. A lot of non disabled people struggle with the idea that disability is not sickness, but within the disability movement, there are also a ton of sick and chronically ill disabled people. And all of those struggles and fights to be seen in the world, I think, are separate from this contemporary focus on wellness, which is New Age spiritualism blended with fitness,

NOTE:
The captions for this feature have been written as image descriptions.

(previous) Alice Sheppard, a multiracial Black woman with curly blonde hair, is photographed in black and white in an empty studio. She is pictured in profile, diving toward the ground while dancing in her wheelchair. Her arms are extended behind her and she is holding crutches.
(above) Sheppard leans forward from her wheelchair with her arms outstreched and fingers splayed.

Hair & Makeup: Avery Golson

(below)　　　Sheppard, smiling, leans forward in her wheelchair. Her crutches are extended before her, creating the shape of an arc.

blended with whatever diet.

LB: How would you feel if dance was taken away from you tomorrow?

AS: I would be devastated, but I would survive. I'm endlessly fascinated by the body and my experience of it. We live in these things and they do stuff and they feel stuff and they respond or don't respond. That relationship with the body is incredible. Dance has shown me how to pay attention to it. If I'm not performing choreographed movements on stage, I'm still interpreting the movement in the streets and I'm still feeling the world through my body—we all do. Even if we took away the lights and the stage and formal training of it all, the body doesn't go away.

LB: Was there ever a point in your life where you didn't listen to your body?

AS: I'm *always* not listening to my body! As dancers, we're supposed to simultaneously listen to our bodies at every moment and then ignore the responses. "It hurts!" Keep going. "I'm tired!" Keep going. I have watched the mainstream dance world wrestle with that. With Kinetic Light, I hope to create space where we can do incredibly beautiful work in body-sustainable ways.

LB: How do you create an environment where you can push yourself as a dancer, but also take care?

AS: I think that's a fundamental problem [for professional dancers] and, in particular, for disabled dancers. You don't have to push your body to its limits. That's not what dancing is. Let's step outside that frame and think about dance as the expression of the body. You don't have to push it to its limits, you don't have to do anything with it. It's not even about controlling your body—because disabled folks know that control. Kinetic Light does physically demanding work, but it's about spending time with your body prior to rehearsal. The trick is to build the body. Not in terms of muscular strength, but to explore and know your body so you can train it. Understanding where your body is, understanding what it likes to do. Then doing the support work to strengthen and care for it as it's doing what you want it to do. For some people, support and care are

going to mean hours in the gym. For others, support and care look like going to two or three dance classes and really investing in mainstream dance education. For others it is none of the above.

LB: All members of Kinetic Light are disabled artists. As you navigate the body and explore themes of disability, race and queerness in your collaborative work, how do

you make sure that everybody on the team is heard?

AS: We are a small team and these collaborators have really strong artistic voices. One of the metaphors we use is "This is like a bunch of wild horses." I am learning how to usher the horses in one direction. Laurel [Lawson; dancer/technology lead/choreographic collaborator], Jerron [Herman; dancer/choreographic collaborator] and Michael [Maag; scenographer] are incredible artists. So the question here is what serves the work? How is that best expressed? The non disabled world tends to expect medical stories or stories of personal hardship as the only kind of work disabled people make. But it isn't. There is tremendous freedom in being able to choose what you stage. You don't always have to be on stage performing somebody else's expectation of your own disability, race or queer trauma.

LB: What's your showtime self-care routine?

AS: I have a longstanding practice, so it's not disconnected from the way I live. There's not just a certain diet that

appears because suddenly there's a show. It's because there is a practice of training, eating, working and sleeping in these ways.

LB: Do you need to decompress after a show?

AS: It takes a long time to come down from a performance. And then after the touring run, there's a big crash.

LB: What does that crash look like?

AS: I have learned to care for myself; to care for my body at the end of the show so that I can do tomorrow's show. We're not staying out until one o'clock in the morning and partying, because we have got to go home and take care. I ice everything, stretch it out, heat pad it up and have a proper meal, because I'm not eating solid meals before the show. There's also a recognition that the energy postshow does not stop just because the curtain has closed.

LB: Do you try to ease the adrenaline out?

AS: You don't want to maintain adrenaline all night, because you won't sleep. Part of it is to let the body process it and come down from the show at its own pace. And then you learn to ride the feelings that come with that. Don't jam a lot of sugar or alcohol into your body postshow. Learn how to ride the coming down and who to be with for postshow vulnerability.

LB: Here's something I have always wanted to ask a professional dancer: Are your friends intimidated to go out dancing with you?

AS: Totally! But that was before I was a disabled dancer. I loved going out to dance. I would dance for hours on end, getting wilder and wilder by the hour. It was all about the movement—faster, higher, sexier, sweatier. I would lose track of who I was; it seemed like I could be anyone or anything. Now, I save my fun dancing for parties, friends or moments in the street. Clubs are too much. Even if the club is accessible, there's not enough floor space to really let go; people are always bumping into me or spilling their drinks in my face.

LB: When you dance for fun, what do you dance to?

AS: This is the dance equivalent of singing in the shower, yes? Anything '80s! What do professional singers sing in the shower, I wonder?

(above)   Sheppard sits on her feet, her arms and crutches extended upward. The image is blurred.

(below)   Sheppard looks down toward her crutch, which she holds by her chest in her right hand. She holds the other crutch over her head with her left arm.
(opposite)   Sheppard's wheelchair is parallel to the ground as her torso curves back and she looks upward.

SOBRIETY
with

Words
ELLIE AUSTIN

On the life-enhancing
potential of not drinking alcohol.

JULIA BAINBRIDGE

Photography
EMMA TRIM

Julia Bainbridge's official title is writer and author but it's also fair to describe her as a trendsetter. Long before the pandemic brought conversations about the impact of social isolation to the fore, the former *Bon Appétit* editor was the creator and host of *The Lonely Hour*, an interview-based podcast about loneliness and solitude.

She was similarly prescient when it came to the rise of sober and sober-curious living. A few years ago, Bainbridge set off on a road trip across America to interview bartenders, drink experts and chefs and to discover unusual and delicious alcohol-free mixed beverages. The result was *Good Drinks*, a compendium of nonalcoholic recipes aimed at anyone rethinking their relationship with alcohol for whatever reason. (Bainbridge doesn't drink alcohol and has previously described herself as coming from "a long line" of people with alcohol use disorders.) Now training to become a therapist, she eventually hopes to integrate her various areas of interest with the goal of helping her readers and clients "reorganize the way" they live and work.

ELLIE AUSTIN: Is there a common thread to your work on loneliness and sobriety?

JULIA BAINBRIDGE: That's hard to answer. I do think, looking back at the past decade of my professional life, I see somebody who wants to make people feel less alone. *The Lonely Hour* podcast was ultimately about the acceptance of loneliness as part of the human condition.

EA: How do you define loneliness?

JB: I think it's this sense of unmooring. Isolation is a pretty objective measure of how many people are around you. Loneliness is subjective. It's a feeling. I also believe loneliness is at the root of addiction, depression, stress, anxiety,

Bainbridge lives in a former candy factory in Brooklyn with her partner, the chef Alan Delgado.

and our struggle to feel that we matter.

EA: How would you describe your relationship with sobriety today?

JB: For shorthand, I say I'm sober, but where appropriate, I take the time to explain that while I don't drink alcohol, I do consume other intoxicants. I'm very, very about cannabis. It's important to watch that too [although] I don't know if I believe in addictive personalities. I guess it was around 2014 to 2015 when I really started reckoning with my relationship with alcohol. Serendipitously, that happened at a time when more energy was put into alcohol-free beverages. For someone whose job it was to go out and see what was happening in restaurants, it was impossible not to notice that something was happening.

EA: There are so many terms to describe drinks that don't contain alcohol: soft drinks, mocktails, virgin, zero proof. Does it matter how we refer to them?

JB: I've seen so many stabs [at different phrasing]. "Mocktail" does a good job of saying what it is in one word. We all know that we're not talking about juice. We're talking about something at the next level that doesn't have alcohol. I also understand all the funny feelings around "mocktail" as it's kind of mocking something else. It's defined by its absence. The title of my book, which I really fought for, is *Good Drinks*. Witnessing all the anxiety around coming up with a proper term, I thought, "They're just drinks. I'm done with the conversation." And also, I guess it was meant to subvert when we say to a friend or a colleague, "Hey, do you want to go out for a drink after work?" It's presumed that it's an alcoholic one.

EA: That's true. In certain social situations,

(opposite)   For *Good Drinks*, Bainbridge traveled around the US and met bartenders creating complex, sophisticated nonalcoholic drinks.

128   WELL-BEING

WELL-BEING

"Alcohol is the only drug you have to justify not taking. That is changing."

there has traditionally been a stigma attached to not drinking. Is that changing?

JB: Someone, I forget who, said alcohol is the only drug you have to justify not taking. That is changing ... but I am wary of a lot of the conversation about changes in drinking behavior based on anecdotal evidence. It can feel like something is happening more than it actually is. There's no doubt that there are more [nonalcoholic] products on the market than ever before. More people are participating in things like Dry January. But I also saw data just published a couple of days ago that showed alcohol-related deaths were up from 2015 to 2019. I think it's sometimes irresponsible—the way in which people talk about this shift in drinking behavior that's based on your handful of friends in New York who found themselves drinking too much during the pandemic and decided to seek out other options.

EA: So the sobriety movement risks being co-opted by affluent young professionals as just another wellness trend?

JB: Do I think that's the case when we're talking about how the lifestyle media has talked about this movement? Yes. I would love to figure out a way to write a book or a pamphlet, even something free online, of delicious, alcohol-free drinks made up of three ingredients you can find at the grocery store. My book is only going to serve a certain set of people with the resources to source all these expensive, hard-to-find ingredients. And there are plenty of people who have come to their sobriety through an alcohol use disorder who are totally triggered by the accoutrements used to make an alcohol-free cocktail in my book—mixing glasses, a jigger.

EA: Are there different ways to approach sobriety depending on whether you're giving up alcohol because of addiction issues as opposed to a desire for better general health?

JB: I don't give advice. I'm not a medical professional or a scientist. I don't work in the recovery field. I just think we have to be careful not to lump together the sober curious and those in recovery. We should be careful about co-opting language used in recovery to sell alcohol-free products. Maybe I'm too prickly around this. I don't know.

EA: Have you noticed any trends around gender and sobriety? Are men more harshly judged for giving up alcohol than women, for example?

JB: I don't exactly have an answer but if anything, I would say that, because historically there has been more social stigma attached to women consuming alcohol than men, maybe there is less stigma attached to not drinking for women. In the 1800s, alcohol use for women was linked to promiscuity, sexual misconduct, neglect of children. In the 1920s, women protested patriarchal attitudes by drinking publicly and proudly but society's view didn't really change.

EA: Going back to loneliness, what are your personal strategies for dealing with sadness or feelings of disconnection?

JB: I don't try to fix it or combat it. The most profound way in which my [podcast] guests influenced my understanding of loneliness was through their underscoring of its merits. The poet and philosopher David Whyte talks about loneliness as "a doorway to becoming." He would say, "Try and see it as a place for understanding yourself and then step off from it." I would say that's true, when I think of my guests' stories. Loneliness told people where they needed to go. It can be oddly nourishing if you can make your way through it.

EA: Aside from sobriety and loneliness, are there any other social issues you want to delve into?

JB: I'm drawn to our elder people. As a rule, I have stopped dyeing my hair. I'm never going to fuck with my face. At one point, I really wanted to make porn with older, mature actors. Even the men I know who you would say are progressive, they're attracted to all different kinds of body sizes and races but when it comes to women of a certain age they're just like, "Stop." Youth and beauty are inextricably linked and there is so much to say about that.

Essay:

TOO MUCH OF A GOOD THING

Words
ANNABEL BAI JACKSON

When I was a college student, there would be a five-day period each term labeled "wellness week." The student committee would organize tai chi classes, advertise 6 a.m. group runs and give out "smoothie shots" in the cafeteria. I petted alpacas, I attended relaxation webinars, I even had a session of craniosacral therapy, in which I was informed that my body, impassively sprawled across the massage table, had "a good energy." In these moments, the sensation of well-being—wrapped up in the languages of both discipline and recuperation—was seductive. A future fanned out before me: exercise at sunrise, probiotics at noon, meditation at night. Like most people, I didn't have the discipline to turn these tasters into an actual routine. But for some, the belief in regimen as the path to renewal can become an obsession. As the wellness industry booms, and the aesthetic

The irony of this trajectory is striking but perhaps it was always inevitable. Well-being—the general state of happiness and good health—often gets subsumed into the image-conscious, commercially driven notion of *wellness*. Deriving from physician Halbert L. Dunn's 1961 book, *High Level Wellness*, the concept rejects the neutral state of "unsickness" as a health ideal. Instead, according to Dunn, we should be in positive, active pursuit of elevation through continuous acts of "maximizing the potential of which the individual is capable."[2] Wellness is always in the present tense. "*Maximizing* is a dynamic word, a *becoming* word," Dunn writes. But how far can we maximize—and what kind of ideal do we want to become?

"Wellness is often associated with an element of evangelism," says Renee McGregor, sports dietician and author of *Orthorexia: When Healthy*

" Wellness is always in the present tense. But how far can we maximize—and what kind of ideal do we want to become?"

demands placed upon our bodies become borderline impossible to achieve, healthy habits such as exercising regularly and eating a balanced diet can turn into fixations. Disorders like orthorexia (the obsession with eating "pure" foods) and exercise dependency are increasingly recognized among mental health professionals.[1] These conditions have yet to appear in the Diagnostic and Statistical Manual of Mental Disorders (DSM), America's handbook of classified mental health disorders, but first-person testimony reveals the true anguish of obsession. Search through online forums and you'll find stories of individuals guilt-ridden for missing a gym class, or self-proclaimed "skincare addicts" on Reddit asking, "Is there any benefit to sunlight?" Overwhelmed by the ever more granular, ever more exacting subtleties of health and self-care, the drive to be well can produce its own distinctive form of *un*wellness.

Eating Goes Bad. In her book, McGregor points out the Greek origins of the word—ortho coming from the prefix meaning "correct"—and notes the loss of objectivity entailed in the disorder: "Reducing saturated fat can easily, over time, become eliminating all fat ... increasing vegetables can become eating only vegetables." The book covers cases such as that of Jordan Younger, the gluten-free, sugar-free, oil-free, grain-free, legume-free, plant-based raw vegan whose wholesome blog posts veiled dangerously disordered eating. After her hair fell out, her periods stopped and her skin took on an orange tinge from overconsumption

(1)   Although orthorexia is not a stand-alone condition in the DSM-5, it meets the criteria for an avoidant/restrictive food intake disorder (ARFID) which is a recognized condition.

(2)   Dunn's coinage was slow to catch on. In a 2010 article for *The New York Times*, Ben Zimmer recalls a 1979 *60 Minutes* segment on the topic in which the host began by saying: "Wellness: There's a word you don't hear every day." Zimmer goes on to point out that, in fact, many people now hear that word multiple times a day.

of sweet potatoes, Younger pivoted to raising awareness of the danger of extreme diets.[3] Many of her stories center on the impact of social media, which often features wellness's powerful visual shorthand—rainbow-flecked poke bowls and yoga poses at sunset—in a way that's influential and irresistible.

McGregor also writes about a teenage girl she treated, whose recovery from a sugar-free, soy-free and low-fat vegan diet stalled because she "chose to believe what she was reading on the Internet." It's through social media that the internet replicates wellness's anxiety of *becoming*. You don't see influencers execute a task just once: You witness them perform it over and over again, reminding us that it's a lifestyle, rather than just a product, that we're buying into.

" It's very common to be obsessed with the body, as if it's this thing we can manipulate and decorate."

Not everyone with an Instagram account who wants to improve their well-being falls into the trap of wellness obsession. The risk of doing so is partly down to personality type. "Most people who develop a dangerous relationship with food and exercise tend to be type A," McGregor writes—that is, high achievers who often have a greater propensity for stress. "If you put this person in the right psycho-social space, [one] that is a competitive environment with societal ideals, this creates the perfect storm to allow for dysfunctional behaviors to develop." People with exercise dependency, for instance, might spend three to four hours each day in the gym on their workouts—an act that fosters an often illusory sense of control over everyday life.[4] "It's never about food, body, or

(3)   Although she has changed her branding from The Blonde Vegan to The Balanced Blonde, Younger still posts about a wide range of wellness solutions. Her website includes affiliate links to a juicer, probiotic supplements, ketamine therapy and coffee enema bags.

(4)   The Priory, a private addiction rehab and mental health hospital in the UK, defines exercise addiction on its website as the point at which "the basic enjoyment of exercise and the knowledge that you are improving your health is overtaken by a psychological dependence on exercise which can result in injury and illness."

exercise," McGregor says. "This is just the means by which the individual is trying to void the discomfort around low self-worth."

Why the body, in particular, falls prey to these feelings comes down to its plasticity. "It's very common in our culture to be obsessed with the body, as if it's this thing we can manipulate and decorate," Peach Friedman, yoga instructor and author of *Diary of an Exercise Addict*, tells me.[5] Some students in Friedman's yoga classes zone in on the physical discipline of the practice, asking her which poses will help them lose weight or tone up. This fixation on regulating their bodies is part of "a very long checklist: you need to get eight to nine hours of sleep at night, you need to wake up early with the sun, you need to have your lemon water, you need to do your yoga." If they can achieve this, the belief system goes, "then they will be better—then they will be more worthwhile."

How can we develop a positive relationship with our bodies, then, that doesn't rely on the false positivity of "resetting," "glowing" and "enhancing"? We can separate well-being from the hyper-discipline of wellness, first by recognizing just how much of life's texture is lost to its obsessions. The purgative, controlling language of toxic wellness—*shred, tone, purify, cleanse*—is anathema to the occasional excess, risk and pleasure that often lead to a more holistically positive life experience. Friedman, who had a diagnosed eating disorder alongside her exercise addiction, says, "I did not have a lot of access to pleasure—whether it be the pleasure of eating, sex or anything sensual," at the height of her illness. "We want life to have richness, but we limit that when we over-control our experience. And we really lose wellness."

Psychologists have drawn similar conclusions. In 2003, Professor Robert J. Vallerand made the distinction between "harmonious passion" and "obsessive passion." Harmonious passion occurs when an individual chooses to engage in an activity, freely and autonomously, and in doing so experiences an authentic positive effect. Obsessive passion, by contrast, claims the individual as its own: They feel an overwhelming, internalized pressure to engage, perceiving their identity to be at stake in the activity. Those with an obsessive passion for sports are, unsurprisingly, at a higher risk of exercise dependency, with obsessive passion classified as a "strong indicator" for possible addiction.

It's easy to see that obsessive passion play out in the excesses of the wellness movement. As the academics Carl Cederström and André Spicer write in *The Wellness Syndrome*, the "ideology" of mainstream wellness requires the individual to be "potent, strong-willed and relentlessly striving to improve herself": eternally captain of ship, master of fate.[6] Even for those of us who don't develop dangerous fixations, this ideology is exhausting and unsustainable. Turning to harmonious passion in the pursuit of well-being entails a different set of values: choice, freedom and finding one's own path to contentment. Harmonious passion requires the acceptance of contingency—breaking down the equivalence between discipline and value, identity and activity.

It also means finding the courage to reject the now ubiquitous wellness idiom. "To step away and say, 'I'm going to set my own standards for well-being,' is very counterculture," says Friedman.

(5)   Friedman's book is a memoir of her experiences as a turn-of-the-millennium college senior who dealt with a bad breakup by running 10 miles a day and often consuming only 800 calories. She lost a third of her body weight in three months.

(6)   *The Wellness Syndrome* follows people with extreme passions, which includes diet obsessives but also people who are fixated on the "quantified self," monitoring their own health metrics, including their bowel movements, as well as their sleep and step count.

Mind

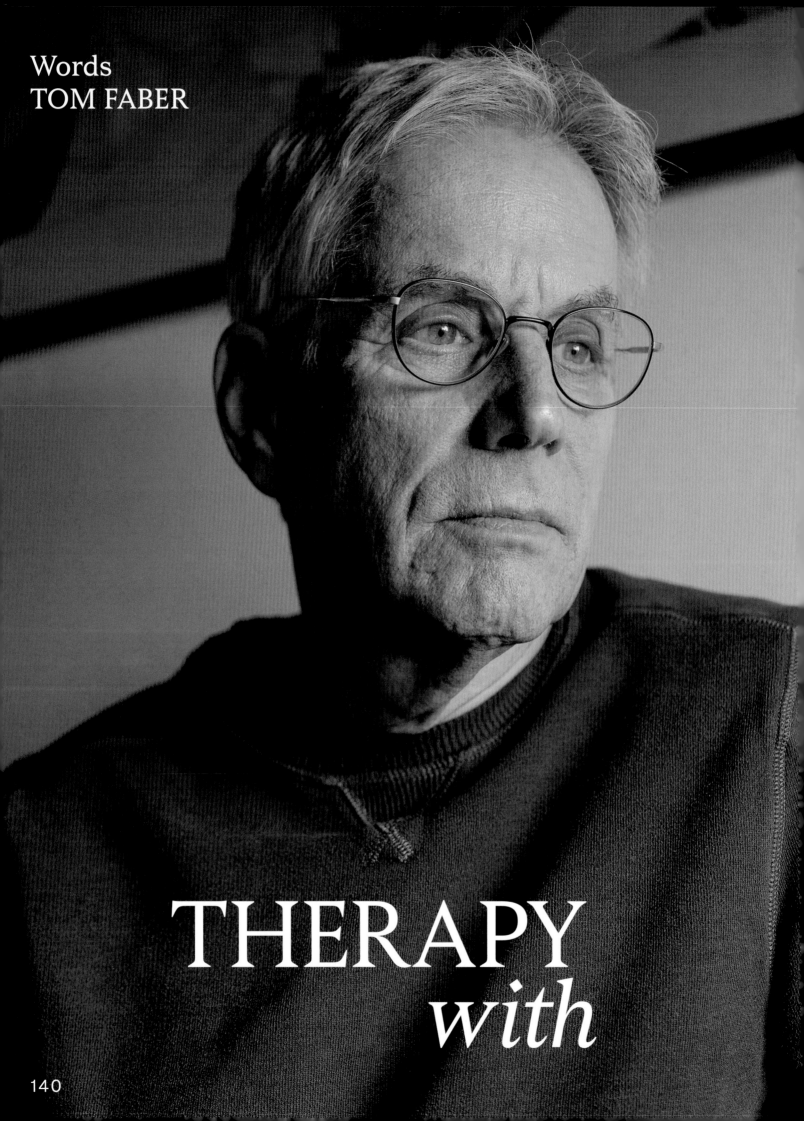

THERAPY
with

Everyone carries scars from their own life.
Gay men also carry those of their community. From his
practice in Berkeley, clinical psychologist and author
WALT ODETS is working to help people heal.

Photography
CAYCE CLIFFORD

WALT
ODETS

"I haven't lived my life around these losses but I'm a different person for it all."

One of the first things you realize when reading Walt Odets' book is that he must be an exceptional therapist. *Out of the Shadows: Reimagining Gay Men's Lives*, published in 2019, collates the author's insights and recollections from over 35 years of providing therapy to a clientele of gay men through the AIDS epidemic and its long aftermath. Odets, who describes the book as his "swan song," is sensitive, probing and humane in his exploration of the psyche, at times encouraging the acceptance of ambiguities and at others disarmingly opinionated. The book feels all the more important since there are surprisingly few mainstream psychological resources specifically aimed at gay men. On release, *The New York Times* heralded it as "poignant and achingly beautiful."

Alongside his writing and therapy, Odets has long been an advocate for HIV awareness, writing an influential book in 1995 about the psychological trauma—the grief, anxiety and survivor's guilt—suffered by gay men who had not contracted the virus. He is now 76, with neatly combed gray hair and dark-rimmed glasses, and still practices therapy part time from his home in Berkeley. As a gay man himself, Odets includes reflections on his own romantic history in one of the book's most lyrical sections, chronicling a shifting constellation of multiple romantic partners that exemplifies the unconventional shapes that meaningful, functioning gay relationships can take.

The world has changed a lot for gay people since he began, especially for the young, white, cisgender gay men who grow up in accepting families under broadly supportive governments. Yet the community continues to suffer today from many of the issues explored in this book. Despite outward signs of gay self-acceptance such as Pride parades and marriage, Odets rightly emphasizes the damage still wrought by internalized shame—a creation of the stigma projected onto gay men by their families, religions and wider society. Odets' wisdom and experience on the path to self-acceptance are relevant and revelatory for anybody, regardless of sexuality or age.

TOM FABER: You write that gay men are far more likely to be in therapy than straight men. Why is this?

WALT ODETS: I've heard some people say that they knew they were gay from the age of five—what they mean is they could feel they were different from other people; they didn't feel like they belonged. Trying to find yourself, sort your emotions and figure out how you relate to other people is very hard without therapy.

TF: One prominent idea in your book is that there's a difference between calling someone "homosexual" and calling them "gay." Can you explain this?

WO: When you define someone as

homosexual, you're just talking about sex. Gay people are defined by more than this: It's who they attach to, who they love. Some people have sex with no real interest in each other, sure, but after a while they develop an emotional attachment to someone. Sex is simply an expression of that attachment, not its foundation.

TF: You've worked with gay men most of your life. How much progress do you think the community has made in that time?

WO: In the USA, it depends a lot on where you are. I'd guess that a majority of the country still don't support gay people.

TF: But there is tangible progress— like gay marriage, anti-discrimination legislation and antiretroviral drugs which treat HIV.

WO: True, but I don't know what percentage of people are supported by those changes. There are many people in the US who still can't afford antiretroviral drugs. I think they should be handing them out on the sidewalk. Meanwhile people from minority groups are still not getting adequate treatment.

TF: How much did the AIDS epidemic shape your career?

WO: It affects my work even today. Of my 16 current patients, four of them carry HIV. One found out at the age of 28, back when they didn't say: "You're HIV positive," they said: "You're dying." He's never gotten over that, he still feels like he's going to die from it. He's a very thoughtful, intelligent guy, but he can't shake it because it has become part of his identity. At the height of the epidemic in the 1990s, the death rate in San Francisco was almost 50% of the gay population. That's a lot of people. There was a time I did a weekly therapy group with HIV-positive physicians, but it became unbearable to me after a while. In a group of eight, four died in one week. The other four came in and said: "Where's Todd?" and "I haven't seen

Odets runs his private psychology practice in Berkeley, California, where the majority of his clients are gay men.

Jim here," and I had to tell them they had died. They sat there crying, they ran out of the room—and these were people who wanted to take care of others, to make people's lives better.

TF: Do these losses leave lasting psychological scars?

WO: Yes. AIDS didn't just affect my career, it left me and many other people with a kind of despair. I talk in my book about losing my partner Robb, whom I loved deeply. That's a loss that I'll never recover from. I have experienced maybe 10 or 11 hideous deaths—the first was when my mother died when I was seven years old. I remember when my father told me, I didn't cry but I slipped into a kind of fog. I felt like I was going down a well, just quietly sliding down, and I don't think I ever crawled out of that. It's simply too much of a loss. I haven't lived my life around these losses but I'm a different person for it all. I don't pack these feelings up in the closet.

TF: With the advances in antiretroviral medicine which can help people with HIV live long, healthy lives and the introduction of the preventive medication PrEP, many people might assume that AIDS is a thing of the past, particularly in the West. How do you feel about that?

WO: It's ridiculous because people still need medical care and helpful medications should be given away by the government, like they do with COVID-19.

TF: Humans can suffer from many things, but your book focuses on shame. What can we do to disarm our shame?

WO: I think therapy is very helpful. It doesn't have to be professional, it could be a couple of friends who are open and insightful. Shame is very disruptive, not just because it limits your life, but because it makes you feel inadequate. Of course, the experience of this and how to treat it will be different for every person.

(opposite)   Odets' first book, *In the Shadow of the Epidemic: Being HIV-Negative in the Age of AIDS*, was published by Duke University Press in 1995.

TF: What would you like people to take away from your book?

WO: I'd like them to be able to think about themselves without feeling they're in conflict with other people or society. I get hundreds of long emails from people who have read the book, who talk about how they personally related to it. I'm very moved by them. I respond to every one.

TF: Do you have a sense that gay men are constantly in a battle with society or with themselves?

WO: A lot of them feel that way, particularly when the family treats them badly. I often see that when the family is immediately accepting of the gay child, that this is very helpful. If you can find acceptance in the family, it prevents a lot of emotional damage.

TF: What would an ideal world look like in terms of sexuality? Would everyone just be human and love whoever they want without being labeled? Or rather a world where people use labels but they're respected for their choices?

WO: It's more likely to be the latter, but the first is more important. I have many friends for whom it has no bearing that I'm gay. I also had relationships with women early on, but I never attached to them the way I did to other men.

TF: So the ideal would be a world where nobody puts themselves in a box and they could all sleep with whoever they wanted?

WO: Sure, why not?

TF: Might that spell the end of queer culture as its own discrete tradition?

WO: I think you have a point there—but we haven't got close enough to see that yet.

TF: In your book you write: "Our choice is simple. We can either be ourselves or be ourselves pretending to be something else." As a closing thought, why is self-acceptance so important?

WO: To feel you're somehow deficient impairs a life. Self-acceptance doesn't come from just deciding you're fine and don't want to think about it. It can only come from working at who you want to be, how you express yourself and how this fits into your connections with other people. It's about honestly understanding who you are.

" To feel you're somehow deficient impairs a life."

Inside the astrology company
on a mission to prove workplace well-being is
more than a corporate tagline.

CHANI NICHOLAS

Words
JENNA MAHALE

and
SONYA PASSI

Photography
KOURTNEY KYUNG SMITH

At the very minimum, working full-time at Chani Inc.—the LA-based tech company behind the popular two-year-old astrology app Chani—will guarantee you a salary of $80,000. This figure, according to co-founder and CEO Sonya Passi, is "a wage that you can actually afford to live on in an expensive city." "There's so much noise about what wellness is," she says. "For us, wellness is fundamentally rooted in an understanding that you cannot be well if you're not financially secure." Chani's commitment to workplace well-being goes far beyond the lip service paid by most companies. Employee provisions include unlimited vacation, unlimited menstrual leave and the offer of a $2,000 wealth-building stipend. "We wanted to carve out a specific amount of money that was there for you to just invest in your future," Passi explains. Her wife and co-founder, the eponymous astrologer Chani Nicholas, who is president of Chani Inc., agrees. "You can't be well unless your communities are also well," she says. Nicholas tells me that 5% of the app's annual revenue is disbursed as cash grants to domestic violence survivors via the nonprofit FreeFrom.org, which Passi founded in 2016.

JENNA MAHALE: How do you think being in a relationship and running a business affects the workplace you aim to create?

SONYA PASSI: It's a relationship that is rooted in trust and shared abundance. I think that then permeates everything that we do, and allows us to bring the best of both of us to the work and to the team and to the company. It's a lot of fun. It's very easy to talk things through when your business partner is your wife.

CHANI NICHOLAS: We're deeply intense people, so everything we do is with a tremendous amount of thought and processing, and we've always been engaged with the idea of the most thoughtful, healing-from-the-inside-out way to build a tech company: How do we create a workplace where people feel like they have autonomy, power and the resources they need to live?

As well as running a business together, Nicholas and Passi are married and expecting their first child.

JM: What does financial well-being mean to you?

CN: To me, financial well-being means that you're able to pay for your housing, your healthcare, your food, things like therapy or any kind of healing session. You're able to buy the books and take the courses that will help you feel fulfilled intellectually, spiritually and emotionally, and you're able to take

time off in a way that feels spacious. You feel like being on vacation isn't going to impact you in a negative way.

JM: I read recently that workers with unlimited vacation time can often end up taking less of it than workers who are given a specific amount. How have you navigated that policy at Chani?

SP: We really want to incentivize people to take that vacation, so we have a vacation stipend that's a use-it-or-lose-it every year. No one wants to say, "Wow, I had $1,500 to spend on travel and I didn't take a holiday." So you can use that for anything—from flights to hotels to car rentals—as long as you are leaving the city that you're in, and *you* are on the vacation, you're not paying for someone else's vacation. We also have a policy where the office closes for six weeks every year, meaning we're all off.

JM: How do you see employees use things like the tech stipend, or the personal and professional growth stipend, and how much do you offer for each of those?

SP: The tech stipend is $3,500 a year. When you're a tech company, you gotta keep your tech fresh. It's really just money that we're giving to Apple every year to pay for quick phones and quick laptops. The personal and professional growth stipend is used for everything from paying for therapy to leadership coaching. People use it for acupuncture, Reiki, buying books for reading pleasure, gym memberships—any way that you can invest in your growth. So the tech stipend is really just something that allows you to do your work, whereas things like the personal and professional growth stipend, the wealth-building stipend, the vacation stipend, those are really opportunities for you to get more enjoyment out of your life.

(opposite)   Alongside her work at Chani, Sonya Passi is the founder and CEO of FreeFrom, an organization that aims to create financial stability for domestic abuse survivors.

JM: Is venture capital investment what's made that business model possible?

CN: No!

SP: We're fully self-funded. That was very important to us. We wanted to maintain 100% control over our company and we wanted the freedom to run it how we saw fit. It's not like family and friends funded us; the business has funded the business. We just invested the profits back into it. When we set out to build an app, ¡we were¡ a team of four. We had no idea if it was going to be successful at all. But we had built a strong relationship with our audience over the years: It meant that in that first year of the app's life, it was incredibly successful—and profitable, too.

CN: As a company, we're not trying to "go public" or do any of that stuff. I am an astrologer. This company was built because of our passion and belief in the practice of astrology and how deeply it's impacted and helped us. The app was a logical thing to do —we wanted a more accessible way for folks to receive astrology from us—but we're not some tech company trying to go big and sell, or let some other parent companies do whatever they want with people's data.

JM: How can you use astrology in the context of workplace well-being?

SP: Separate from the stipends, we pay for all of our staff to get an astrology reading once a year from any astrologer that they choose. What drew me to astrology was the deep validation of my strengths and the life challenges that I had faced, and continue to face, through my chart. It allows me to more intentionally lean into my gifts, lean into what I'm here to do, and accept the challenges. It ultimately supports everyone's growth as individuals; it's an understanding of their creative potential and what they bring to the table based on their astrology. For example, a lot of companies use Myers-Briggs to understand their team and team dynamics. I always say astrology is a much more personalized and thorough version of Myers-Briggs.

CN: Astrology is a language people can use to talk about what they're working on, what they're struggling with, and what the time frame of this part of their life is like. There are personal transits that are just for ¡individuals¡, and then there are collective transits that we're all going through. If someone at the company is going into their Saturn Return in March, we can all collectively talk about that phase of life or self-development. So it's also a group bonding experience. It allows an opening for us all to be a lot more human.

(left)

Nicholas began her astrology career writing an email to friends and family. Her first job listing, posted in 2018, was for a personal assistant to work a 30-hour, five-day work week that paid $60,000.

Photography
HENRIK BÜLOW

WILD NIGHTS
and

Stylist
CAMILLA LARSSON

Dream. Sleep. Create. Repeat.
It's time to get more imaginative in the bedroom.

DUVET DAYS

Set Designer
TINE DARING

(previous)   Mahany wears a dress by ACNE STUDIOS and shoes by NIKE.
(above)   She wears a bodysuit by ALAÏA and socks by CORGI.

Hair & Makeup: Lasse Pedersen. Model: Mahany Pery at Oui Management. Retouch: Wetouch

(above)   Mahany wears a top by TOTEME. Sleeping bag by NATURLIGVIS.

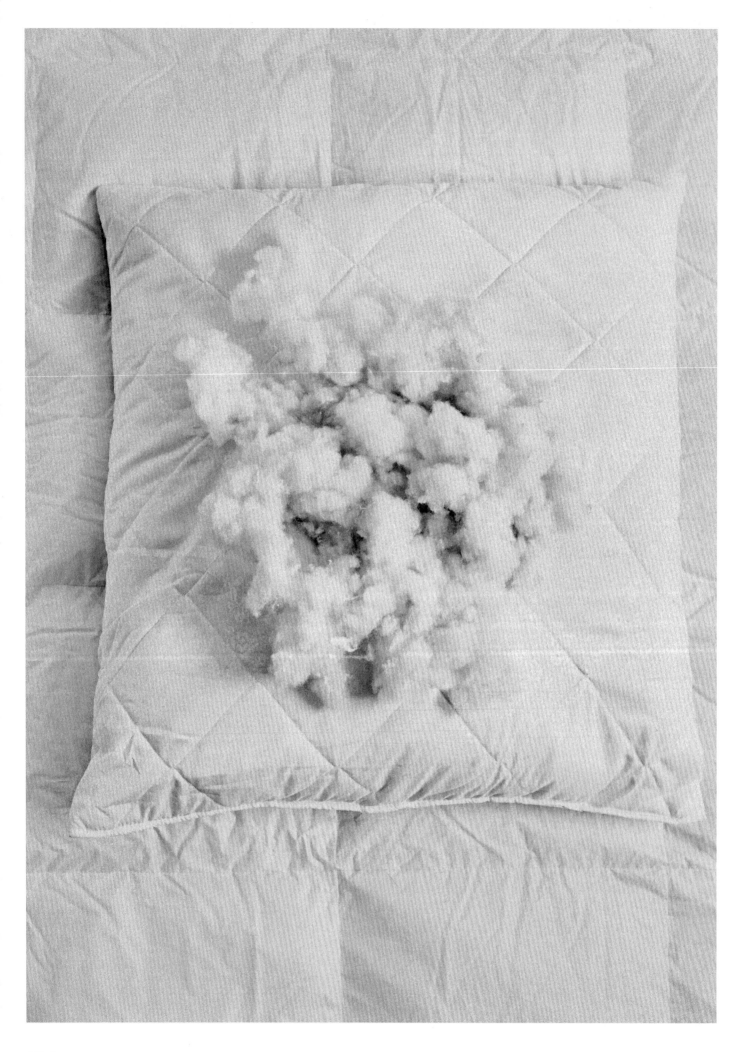

(above)   Mahany wears a top by LOEWE. Cushions by GEISMARS.

(opposite)   Mahany wears a top by TOTEME, trousers by RAINS and boots by WOOD WOOD.

A PICTURE

XIAOPENG YUAN
photographs the world's weirdest
wellness cures.

OF HEALTH

Styling
ZINN ZHOU

Words
ROBERT ITO

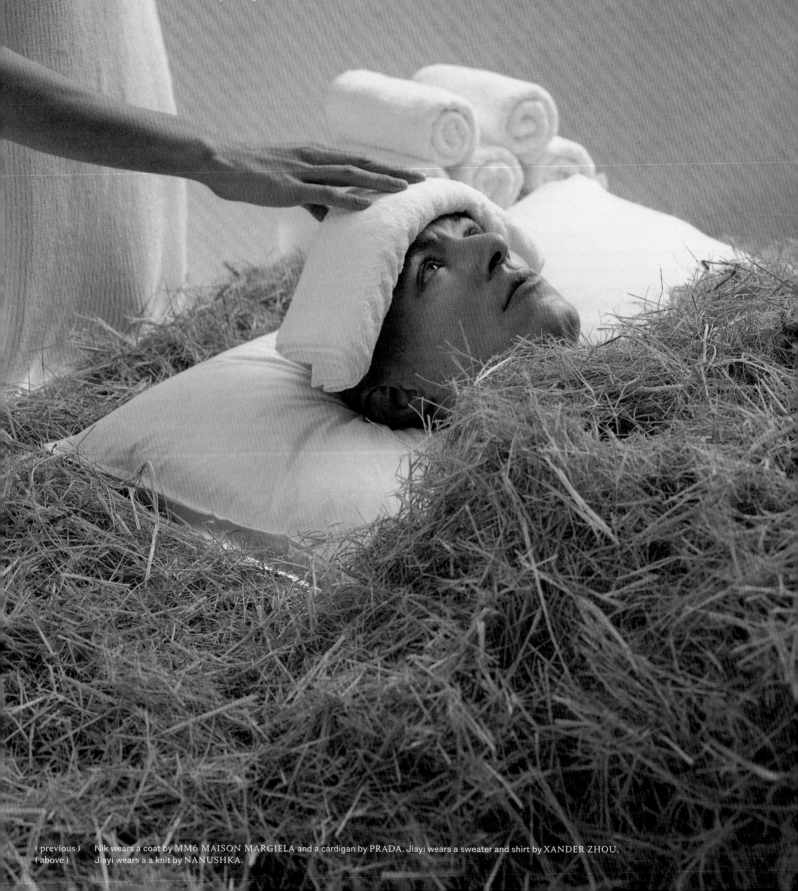

HAY BATHS:

According to northern Italian lore, hay bathing began 300 years ago when local farmers fell asleep in an Alpine meadow in the Dolomites and woke up the following morning miraculously refreshed and pain-free. It must have been that sweet, scratchy hay, they figured, and hay bathing (or, in German, *heubad*) was born. A century ago, practitioners were placed in a pit in the ground and covered in heated heaps of the stuff. Today, spa-goers in Austria and Italy luxuriate in tubs filled with the finest mountain grasses and medicinal herbs, which have been soaked in hot water before-hand. Hay bathers are basically stewing in a tub of hot, wet grass—and no amount of soul-healing lavender and lady's mantle is going to make that sound particularly pleasurable. Even so, fans of the practice swear by it, and claim it can help with a host of ills, from sciatica and rheumatism to obesity and digestive distress.

(previous)   Nik wears a coat by MM6 MAISON MARGIELA and a cardigan by PRADA. Jiayi wears a sweater and shirt by XANDER ZHOU.
(above)   Jiayi wears a a knit by NANUSHKA.

OTONAMAKI:

Otonamaki, literally "adult wrapping," was invented in 2015 by Nobuko Watanabe, a Japanese midwife. In a typical 20-minute session, a person curls into a fetal ball, and is then tied up from head to toe inside of a white cotton mesh sheet. Thus cocooned, the client is rocked back and forth by a therapist, or put in a hammock, or simply placed atop a thin mat and left alone with their thoughts. Years ago, Watanabe observed how parents in Japan were concerned that swaddling their babies might make them claustrophobic, and came up with otonamaki as a way to reassure them it was fine. Along the way, people ended up liking it, and otonamaki is now credited with reducing stress, improving sleep and easing lower back pain. To the skeptical eye, however, otonomaki patients look like they have been trussed up by some backwoods madman, or perhaps wrapped in preparation for a burial at sea.

Hair & Makeup: Ivy Quan. Models: Nik Kosmas and Jiayi. Producers: Abi Chan and Miranda Zheng

(above)   Nik wears a shirt by PRIVATE POLICY, trousers by XU ZHI and shoes by DIESEL.

TOE READING:

Toe reading was created two decades ago by KC Miller, a toe reader and self-described "Instrument of Spirit" based in Tempe, Arizona. While palm readers claim to be able to divine your future by observing the lines and whorls on your fingers and hands, toe readers can tell the sort of person you are (and, consequently, the best person you could be) by looking at the shape, size and relative lengths of your toes. Each toe represents different aspects of your life: Your big toe governs your destiny, but also your spiritual side. Your second toe is connected to communication, so if yours are super long, you should maybe look for a job in public speaking. Sessions combine toe reading with life coaching, which makes toe reading not unlike palm reading and tarot.

VINOTHERAPY:

Depending on whom you ask, vinotherapy—aka "wine baths"—started some time either in the Middle Ages or in the early 2000s. Despite the name, wine bathers are not literally luxuriating in gallons of perfectly good merlot. That would, of course, be obscene. Rather, patrons soak in a bath of warm water to which a carafe or two of wine has been added; in other cases, the water is infused with just the leftovers of the winemaking process: grape seeds, skins, stalks and pulp. (In yet another form of vinotherapy, those same leftovers are added to grapeseed oil and massaged into the skin, acting as exfoliants and leaving one's skin smooth and shiny.) Enthusiasts figure that if drinking red wine (in particular, the heart-healthy polyphenols) is good for you, then bathing in it must be too, but there's little science to back that up.

(opposite)   Nik wears a vest by PRADA and shorts by POUR LUI.

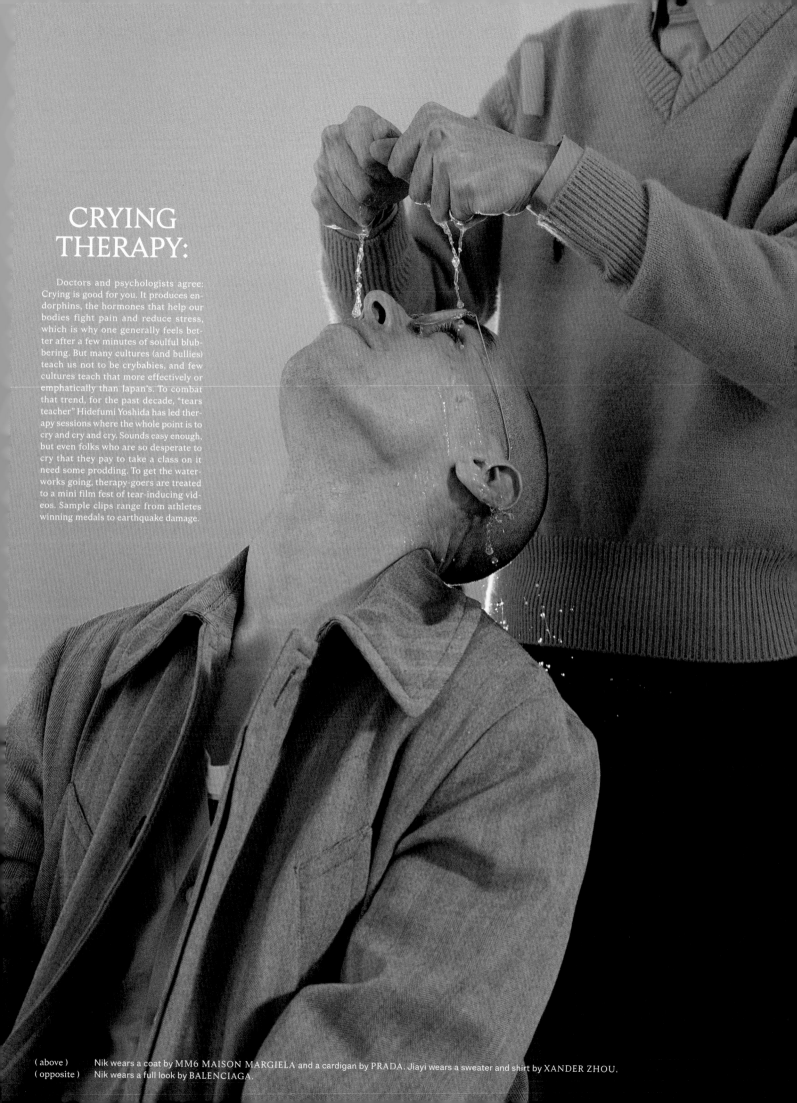

CRYING THERAPY:

Doctors and psychologists agree: Crying is good for you. It produces endorphins, the hormones that help our bodies fight pain and reduce stress, which is why one generally feels better after a few minutes of soulful blubbering. But many cultures (and bullies) teach us not to be crybabies, and few cultures teach that more effectively or emphatically than Japan's. To combat that trend, for the past decade, "tears teacher" Hidefumi Yoshida has led therapy sessions where the whole point is to cry and cry and cry. Sounds easy enough, but even folks who are so desperate to cry that they pay to take a class on it need some prodding. To get the waterworks going, therapy-goers are treated to a mini film fest of tear-inducing videos. Sample clips range from athletes winning medals to earthquake damage.

(above)   Nik wears a coat by MM6 MAISON MARGIELA and a cardigan by PRADA. Jiayi wears a sweater and shirt by XANDER ZHOU.
(opposite)   Nik wears a full look by BALENCIAGA.

FISH THERAPY:

Somewhere at the intersection of "fish will eat just about anything" and "I sure have a lot of dead skin on my feet," fish therapy was born. In a typical spa session, scores of garra rufa—small freshwater fish from Turkey about a half inch long—are placed in a footbath filled with warm water. In go your feet, and instantly, the famished fish swarm. Fish therapy is exactly like a regular pedicure, except instead of a single human buffing your feet with a pumice stone, it's 150 fish sucking the dead skin off of your toes and soles with their tiny, toothless mouths. PETA thinks it's cruel, the Centers for Disease Control and Prevention questions how sanitary it all is and several states in the US ban the practice outright. But your feet, fans say, come out of the experience smooth, tingling and callus-free.

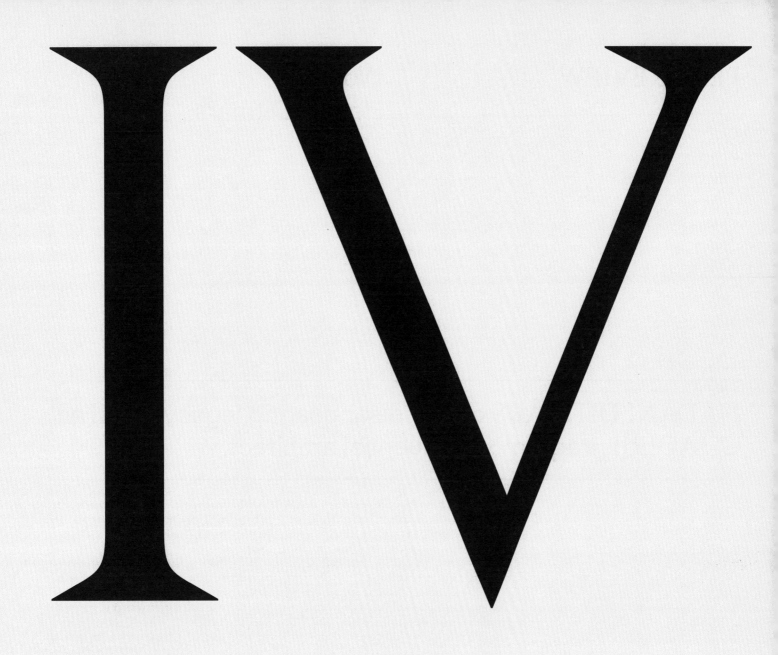

IV

178 — 192

DIRECTORY
Cemeteries, menus and Iraqi modernism.

178	Peer Review	187	Correction
179	Object Matters	189	Last Night
180	Cult Rooms	190	Credits
182	Rachid Koraïchi	191	Stockists
184	Behind the Scenes	192	My Favorite Thing
186	Crossword	—	—

Words:
Hadani Ditmars

HADANI DITMARS on the disappearing legacy of RIFAT CHADIRJI, Iraq's most influential architect.

Rifat Chadirji's architecture was always an unconscious part of my Iraqi travelogues. As his homeland became a part of my inner and outer world over three decades of documenting pre- and post-invasion culture and society, so did his buildings.

Back home in Vancouver, how could I conjure memories of Baghdad without visualizing his Central Post Office? The 1972 classic was looted and damaged after the ill-fated invasion in 2003, but still stands tall as a battle-scarred modernist relic. Or the phantom of his elegant Arch of Ctesiphon–inspired Monument to the Unknown Soldier in Firdos Square, replaced in the early 1980s (as Chadirji photographed its demise) with a statue of Saddam—one that would become a symbol of the invasion when it was toppled by American soldiers. And how could I imagine Mosul without his iconic National Insurance Company building, occupied by ISIS, bombed during "liberation" and then bulldozed in 2018?

Indeed Chadirji's life and work were one with Iraq's spirit and history. Born in 1926, the father of Iraqi architecture and prolific author and photographer designed over a hundred buildings in his homeland in a uniquely Iraqi yet Le Corbusier-inspired take on modernism. Employing a style he called "international regionalism," his work still evokes both ancient and contemporary idioms. Arches and monolithic piers in Chadirji's public work recall regional architecture, while many of his residences employed traditional exteriors integrated with European interiors. As a writer of mixed Middle Eastern and European ancestry currently working on a book about ancient sites and contemporary culture in Iraq, I find his work compelling on many levels.

In 1980, some two decades before I would be expelled from Saddam-era Iraq for writing something that offended the regime, Chadirji was freed from wrongful imprisonment by Saddam, the newly anointed president of Iraq, who assigned him the task of "rebuilding Baghdad" for 1982's Conference of Non-Aligned Nations. It was foiled by the Iran/Iraq war, but not before Chadirji had commissioned prominent architects from the West—including Vancouver's Arthur Erickson whom he visited here in 1983 when he had left Iraq for good—to build some impressive projects.

Chadirji departed this world in 2020 as Iraq erupted into protests against a corrupt system of government—the legacy of the invasion—decades after the mid-century optimism that spawned his career had transformed into widespread ennui and despair. Yet I still share his passion for documenting the ephemeral nature of both modern and heritage Iraqi architecture, as beautiful and fragile as the nation itself, before it disappears.

(1) Ditmars' next book, *Ancient Heart*, is a political travelogue of Iraqi heritage sites and will draw on both her time in the country and interviews, including with Chadirji whom she met in 2016. Her first book, *Dancing in the No-Fly Zone*, recounts her time in Iraq from 1997 until the fall of 2003, covering both pre- and post-invasion life in the country.

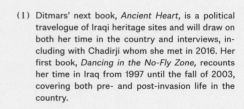

Photo: Paul Taggart

OBJECT MATTERS

Words:
Ed Cumming

An itemized history of the menu.

The story of the menu is entwined with the history of commerce and personal liberty. For most of time, imaginative cooking was something the rich did at home—or, more likely, had done for them. The poor ate what they could get. Inns offered no choice: You ate whatever they had to offer on the day. After hours of traveling by horse or on foot, chances were you were too tired to be fussy anyway. The first inns to offer written options appeared in China around 1100. One example from Hangzhou lists more than 600 dishes. Table service emerged during the same period. Although we get the word *menu* from the French, meaning something small or detailed, they did not appear in France until the late 18th century, after which the practice of providing guests with a bill of fare spread slowly across the continent.

Menus themselves have been seen by some as a mark of capitalist civilization. The US has exhaustive menus; the Soviet Union had "menus" featuring just one item. Menus reflect societal and dietary preferences, as well as design. A new book from Taschen, *Menu Design in Europe*, celebrates their evolving artwork. Children's menus did not appear until children were taken seriously: The Waldorf-Astoria had one in 1921. And until very recently, it was not unusual for elegant restaurants to present women with an unpriced version of the menu, on the assumption they would not be paying.

Today it is standard for Western restaurants to offer vegetarian and vegan menus and to meticulously list allergens and—in some countries—calorie counts. True food obsessives now pride themselves on ordering "off-menu" and it is a selling point for many restaurants to be able to do their customers' bidding.

But the language of menus has escaped the restaurant and been woven into the computer era. There are start-up menus, drop-down menus and endless check-boxes. Online, the world appears as a series of menus: for news, culture, romantic partners. Everything is available. But as restaurants have long known, infinite choice is nearly as bad as none.

Photo: Studio Ingrid Picanyol

CULT ROOMS

Words:
Farah-Silvana Kanaan

In north Lebanon, two architects are rebuilding a corner of OSCAR NIEMEYER'S international fair.

So much in Lebanon has become synonymous with loss. Physical loss, psychological loss, cultural loss. Beautiful buildings have been ravaged first by war, then by greedy corporations. Nowhere is this truer than in Tripoli.[1] A now much-neglected city, it was once known for its craft industries and its Mamluk architecture. In the 1960s, Tripoli was recognized as a cultural hub when it was chosen as the backdrop of the Rachid Karami International Fair, designed by renowned Brazilian architect Oscar Niemeyer.

The construction of the fair, on the outskirts of the city, was abandoned on the brink of completion when the Lebanese Civil War erupted in 1975 and it became yet another ghost in a country haunted by many. Today, the site is surprisingly intact but derelict. In Niemeyer's empty buildings—huge, sculptural and concrete—even the smallest of sounds is echoed back at you.

This began to change in 2018 when the Rachid Karami International Fair was added to UNESCO's World Heritage shortlist. Architects Nicolas Fayad and Charles Kettaneh

of East Architecture Studio won a bid funded by the European Commission to transform one of the site's 15 pavilions, the Guest House, into a design platform and production facility promoting Tripoli's once-great wood industry. A rectangular 10-hectare concrete structure with a windowless facade and an atrium, the Guest House is enveloped on all sides by lush grasses.

Civil war–era scars were inescapable during the renovation process. "The structure was actually occupied by Syrian militias from 1975 to 1990, with clear signs that they tried to keep themselves warm as evidenced by the black deposits all across the ceiling and the scenic space. Graffiti also covered the walls," Fayad recalls. When the architects first entered the site, they had to walk through overgrown nature to access the pavilion.

Fayad and Kettaneh were adamant about two aspects of their design: staying true to Niemeyer's vision and involving local craftsmen in the construction process. The main area houses a wide array of

Photo: © East Architecture Studio

multifunctional spaces in earthy colors, including a material library, a carpentry workshop and a service room for machinery that transforms wood dust into compact bricks.

As graduates of the architecture program of the American University of Beirut, Fayad and Kettaneh were already intimately familiar with the project, and they immersed themselves in Niemeyer's archival prints, searching for clues that would help them honor the structure. They found handwritten annotations by Niemeyer which led them to preserve the timeless monochromatic grayscale approach—using metal rather than aluminum—and focus on flooding the space with light from above by using metal box extrusions and movable lighting spots. The architects believe their transformation of the single-story structure shows the beauty and merits of "adaptive reuse."

They describe the space as "present yet dystopian," a reference not only to Lebanon's past but also to its present. Unfortunately, the project has not yet had the chance to properly flourish as Lebanon—Tripoli, in particular—has been plagued by a dizzying economic downfall, which the World Bank has referred to as "one of the worst in modern history."

What's striking about the Guest House as it stands today is that it not only bridges past and present through its materiality and color scheme, but it also brings the outside in. Overwhelmed by its opaqueness as you approach the building's solid facade, you then enter a space that is flooded with natural light; it's a visceral transformation that you'd hope awaits Lebanon as well.

(1) In October 2019, there was a popular uprising—*thawra*—that briefly returned Lebanon to the hands of the Lebanese people. Citizens took to the streets to protest government corruption and the lack of basic infrastructure services. They celebrated the country's social and religious diversity as a strength rather than a weakness. Nowhere was this as prominent and as joyful as in the northern coastal city of Tripoli, which was soon dubbed the Bride of the Revolution.

© Laurent Boullard. Courtesy of October Gallery/Aicon Gallery

DIRECTORY

RACHID KORAÏCHI

Words:
Daphnée Denis

Meet the Algerian artist building cemeteries.

From artist to gravedigger. That's how Algerian painter and sculptor Rachid Koraïchi describes the evolution of his work. Born in a family of Quranic scholars, Koraïchi puts his faith at the center of his work, exploring spirituality and philosophy through sculpture, painting and calligraphy. For years, he has used his craft to build burial sites for those discarded by society, most recently designing *Garden of Africa* on the shores of Zarzis, Tunisia, where the bodies of migrants who drowned trying to reach Europe wash up routinely.[1] In late 2022, after a migrant ship carrying villagers from Zarzis capsized, and people from the village, including children, were mistakenly buried in unidentified graves at the *Garden of Africa* instead of in the local cemetery, the town's residents profaned the garden's tombs looking for their loved ones—the tragic culmination of political tensions surrounding the site, which had been shortlisted for the Aga Khan Award for Architecture.

DAPHNÉE DENIS: Can you tell me a bit about your family?

RACHID KORAÏCHI: Let's start with my name, Koraïchi. It belongs to the tribe of Muhammad, the Prophet of Islam. On my father's side, my family left Mecca in the seventh century. They built the city of Kairouan in Tunisia, where they created the Blue Quran, one of the most beautiful manuscripts of the Quran in the world. As part of the Sufi order of Tijaniyyah, I grew up surrounded by drawings, calligraphy, carpet weavings, and I'm sure that educated my eye when it comes to the use of color, light and geometric shapes. Learning Arabic [before

Algeria's independence from France] was an act of rebellion. We had to attend French school, but the elders also sent us to Quranic school from the age of five [and] we went to the madrassa. It was nonstop. Already then, I was constantly drawing. I never wanted to be a civil servant, a doctor or even a lawyer, because that would have meant being stuck in an office. I wanted freedom, absolute freedom.

DD: Sufi mysticism infuses your work. How does your artistic practice relate to the divine?

RK: I don't think I can explain it. Mysticism really means mystery. My life appears to be linked to an aesthetic journey; it's a form of prayer, a very long prayer that will last a lifetime. I would never say that I "create" anything, God is the one behind creation.

DD: What does following Sufi philosophy entail?

RK: It means respecting all life: humans, animals, nature. . . . If I saw a spider in my house, I would never kill it. Instead, I would delicately grab it with a Kleenex and put it outside. We don't say we're Sufi—that would be presumptuous, but we choose a certain life journey. I've never drunk a sip of alcohol or taken any drugs even though there's no shortage of that in the art world!

DD: Your latest project, *Garden of Africa*, is both an artwork and a burial site.

RK: It was my daughter—who works for the NGO Action Contre la Faim—who alerted me that in Zarzis, Tunisia, human bodies were being left to rot in a dump. I refused to believe it. When

we went, we were told that the villagers refused to bury migrants in their cemetery. It felt like a nightmare. So we looked for a piece of land to buy. We built a palace for people that were being thrown in a dump. I drew everything on the spot: the surrounding walls, the windows overlooking olive trees, the ceramics, which come from 17th-century Tunis palaces. . . . One by one, we planted plants of paradise like grenade [pomegranate] trees, which symbolize human union, and red bougainvillea, which represent the blood of those who are alive.

DD: Recently, Zarzis residents stormed the garden, opening up the graves to find relatives of theirs who died at sea and were buried there. Are you planning to go back to rebuild it?

RK: I can't go back right now. Even in Paris, I'm receiving threats. I've never seen so much rejection and violence. I wanted to make this site because we, the people of North Africa, keep turning our backs on those from sub-Saharan Africa simply because we have lighter skin. I'm ashamed. If we don't give dignity to the dead, we don't give dignity to those who are alive.

(1) The garden, which was inaugurated in 2021, was laid out according to geometric principles, with the rows between graves ornamented with tiles featuring talismanic glyphs, hearts and other signs. The yellow entrance is set intentionally low so that visitors are obliged to bow respectfully on entering the space.

DIRECTORY

Photo: Ye Rin Mok

Words:
Okechukwu Nzelu

PATRICE WILLIAMS MARKS on the complex, often secret work of publishing's sensitivity readers.

Hundreds of thousands of books are published every year in the US. Alongside the author, most books are nurtured by a skilled team of editors, cover designers, proofreaders, sales executives, production workers and more. Increasingly they are also the product of work by people like Patrice Williams Marks, a sensitivity reader who helps ensure authentic portrayals of marginalized people and experiences.

OKECHUKWU NZELU: How did you get started?

PATRICE WILLIAMS MARKS: I fell into it. I had a group of writer friends, and we would critique each other's material. If they had a Black character, they would ask me if it sounded right. And I would ask the same if I had a character that one of them fit.[1]

ON: How do you find the emotional side of the work?

PWM: One of my first paid reviews was someone whose main character was an older Black man. The character was supposed to be an educated person, but he was using a lot of broken English. All the younger Black characters spoke broken English as well, and most of them were violent. They all were uneducated. And it wasn't just the dialogue, it was the environment [the author] put them in. They all lived in the 'hood. None of them had fathers. I had to keep stepping back because it was so offensive.

ON: Is the work well paid?

PWM: Sensitivity readers are not cheap. An experienced sensitivity reader can charge as much as an editor doing a developmental edit. I make notes on the manuscript and I send them links to articles or videos that explain key points, so it's almost like giving them a research paper. I never negotiate [my fees], but I point people toward other resources, like the database of other sensitivity readers, so that if I can't help them, they can find somebody else.

ON: Are there issues you come across often?

PWM: Describing Black people in reference to food, like chocolate, while the white character has a fully developed backstory and no mention of their skin tone. Another thing that's odd is when authors write elderly Black people: A lot of times they describe them as having an arthritic hand that's frozen. I've come across that over and over again. I also see a lot of what they call "magical Negros," where the person has no backstory, and they're simply there to support the white character.

ON: How does it feel to do work that is not publicly credited?

PWM: I have no problem with it. I give clients an agreement which we both sign. I say that I won't mention their name and their project, and they won't mention my name. There are financial consequences if that's broken. People come to us willingly and I'm not the final say. I give suggestions and the client can do with them what they will. But if the client doesn't take the notes, and then they publish the work and say they had a sensitivity reader, then any criticism of the work would fall back on me.

(1) Sensitivity readers are project specific. For example, author Jodi Picoult, who is white, employed Nic Stone as a sensitivity reader for her 2016 novel *Small Great Things* about a Black nurse who treats the baby of white supremacists. In an interview with *Slate* published the next year, Stone spoke about her own use of a sensitivity reader for a book about a woman with bipolar disorder. She told *Slate* that the reader's involvement had "completely changed the scope" of her book.

FLEXING MUSCLES

Crossword:
Mark Halpin

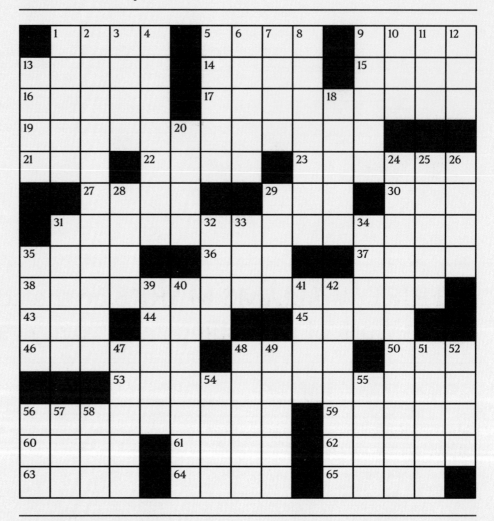

ACROSS

1. TikTok and Tindr, for two
5. Classic fashion designer Cassini
9. Older relative, fondly
13. Deserve
14. Wander widely
15. Affirmative for the masses
16. "I'm here to help!"
17. Like *La Boheme* and *Aida*
19. "This is very much a muscle, at least up until now"?
21. Prefix for center or cycle
22. Ages
23. Says "rrrrrrrrrrrr"
27. Two hands pointing straight up indicate this
29. Inventor Whitney
30. Solo in sci-fi
31. Muscles have fun on a windy day?
35. Casual contraction
36. Covert ops conductors
37. Summers on the Seine
38. The best out of a group of small, young muscles?
43. "Sprechen ___ Deutsch?"
44. The only zodiac sign that can fit in this space
45. Little hoppers
46. Imbue with a spirit
48. Reach one's breaking point
50. 44 Across's month, for short
53. Novel about a muscle's accommodations?
56. Spoils, like milk
59. When prompted
60. One of the Stark girls
61. Name in many an elevator

62. Lecherous looks
63. Fruit-filled desserts
64. Lose vibrancy
65. Piece of cake

DOWN
1. Moral author?
2. Pays for in advance
3. Cotton for high-end shirts
4. Sound systems
5. Hunter that comes out at night
6. Yearns (for)
7. Like many a villain
8. Become unpleasant, like a situation
9. One purported way to lose weight
10. Parisian pal
11. Soup ingredient
12. Advice columnist Landers
13. Source of inspiration
18. Airy entrances
20. Playlist part
24. Béchamel and the like
25. Ensuing
26. '90s gaming console, in brief

28. Bart Simpson's school bus driver
29. Ben Gurion Airport line
31. Stay in bed awhile
32. Tres y cinco
33. Romeo's "Rubbish!"
34. Another purported way to lose weight
35. Chapel recess
39. Botches, as a task
40. Talks about
41. "Dies ____"
42. Of the finest quality, to a Brit
47. Mrs. Chaplin and others
48. Ika and calamari
49. Many a caregiver
51. Unhealthy interest?
52. Thousand-dollar sums, slangily
54. Scintilla
55. Seat in first class, perhaps
56. Use as a resource
57. Psychic Geller
58. Ingredient in a Manhattan or Reuben
—

CORRECTION: THE STARVING ARTIST

Words:
Salome Wagaine

Bad times don't always make for good art.

It is said that great art often has its roots in hard times; that the well of inspiration from which artists and creatives draw in times of economic collapse or social turmoil is far more generous than that available during periods of relative stability and prosperity. But do financial constraints make for finer cultural outputs?

Patronage has had a critical role in the production and ongoing support of fledgling artists. The sponsorship the de Medici family bestowed upon their native Florence and beyond resulted in the erection of the Uffizi Gallery, Michelangelo's painting in the Sistine Chapel and in establishing Florence as the city from which the Renaissance

flowed. Not much has changed in the last five centuries: It was Charles Saatchi's advertising wealth that supported the work of the Young British Artists during the 1990s, for instance.[1]

Outside of private philanthropy, governments have provided fiscal stimuli to artists, such as during Franklin D. Roosevelt's New Deal. A list of the people involved in the initiatives amount to a broad survey of postwar and mid-century American culture: John Steinbeck, Orson Welles, Jackson Pollock, Zora Neale Hurston, Mark Rothko. Each was responding to a particularly dynamic period of history including the emergence of the US as a dominant international superpower and a number of civil rights campaigns and struggles. This context does add some credence to the claim that it is out of what we might call "interesting times" that distinctive art is made. The time during which these artists lived provided a strong backdrop with which they could convey the depth of human emotion and possibility that often marks out significant culture. But it was financial support that gave them the time and means to hone their skills.

The belief that there is a link between precarity and cultural excellence stems from a lingering fear of the indulged artist. Someone who sits aloof and outside the mess of ordinary life, unfamiliar with sacrifice and compromise, the thinking goes, subsequently makes bad, or unmoving work. This worry is not completely unjustified, but a greater threat to artistic promise is a world where success is reserved for those able to withstand financial insecurity.

(1) Although the Young British Artists needed Saatchi as a backer, they did also benefit from the more generalized economic downturn in the early 1990s by opening up group shows in the London factories, warehouses and office buildings that had been sitting empty.

Photo: Philotheus Nisch / Connected Archives

LAST NIGHT

Words:
George Upton

What did New York stylist BEVERLY NGUYEN do with her evening?

Beverly Nguyen says she is both an early riser and a night owl. Much like the famously indefatigable city that she calls home, the stylist needs only a few hours of sleep to balance high-profile fashion shoots with her homewares pop-up, Beverly's. As she explains, when it comes to sleep, it's all about quality, not quantity.

GEORGE UPTON: What did you do last night?

BEVERLY NGUYEN: I arrived in New York from Paris early evening. I have these little rituals when I land. I always go for a run to decompress, and when I get home I make myself an omelet, because I like to re-familiarize myself with my apartment. Then I had an iced coffee and a shot of Viola Mezcal and later went out to a dinner hosted by a good friend.

GU: Do you have a bedtime ritual?

BN: I have a skincare routine, which is a very ritual experience, and I'll have a nightcap if I've been out and I'm still feeling the energy from the party. I put on my pajamas, listen to music and meditate a little—it's just me with my thoughts, thinking about the next day, which I love.

GU: What's your bedroom like?

BN: I am very particular about my bedroom. I'm easily stimulated so it's extremely bare. It's just a bed on the floor, though my sheets, pillows and my duvet are very specific—everything has been strategically studied to induce me into a coma as soon as I lie down. It's a very zen space. I don't have a TV, there's no laptop or phone, and I get up naturally, so I haven't had to set an alarm in years.

GU: What would be your ideal night in New York?

BN: I have a really tight group of friends in New York, so it would be us getting a drink at Fanelli's in SoHo before going back to my house. I would cook a big dinner and we would be around my dining table until two in the morning, just talking and drinking wine.

Photo: Katie McCurdy

CREDITS

COVER:	PHOTOGRAPHER	Michael Oliver Love
	STYLIST	Mandy Nash
	HAIR	Inga Hewett
	MAKEUP	Chloe Hicks
	MODELS	Lehlohonolo Mokele, Jude van Schalkwyk, Liam du Plessis and Robyn Lombard
	LOCATION	Atlantis Dunes, Cape Town
		All models wear looks by SLEEPER from AKJP Studio

BETWEEN US:	MODELS	Candace Redlinghys and Jude van Schalkwyk at My Friend Ned
		Claudia S and Lehlohonolo M at 20 Model Management
		Robyn Lombard at Kult
		Liam du Plessis at Boss
	ENVIRONMENTAL COMPLIANCE OFFICER	Chris Zuidema at ECO Services

WILD NIGHTS AND DUVET DAYS:	STYLING ASSISTANT	Noah Chahid
	PHOTO ASSISTANT	Frederik Kastrupsen

A PICTURE OF HEALTH:	STYLING ASSISTANT	Zoe Haonan
	PHOTO ASSISTANT	Shutong
	LOCATION	303 Art Studio, Shanghai

SPECIAL THANKS:		Mariclare Hulbert

STOCKISTS:
A — Z

A	A.P.C.	apcstore.com
	ACNE STUDIOS	acnestudios.com
	AÉRÉ	aere.dk
	AERON	aeron.com
	AESTHER EKME	aestherekme.com
	AKJP	akjpstudio.com
	ALAÏA	maison-alaia.com
	ANN DEMEULEMEESTER	anndemeulemeester.com
B	BALENCIAGA	balenciaga.com
	BIRROT	birrot.com
C	CARL HANSEN & SØN	carlhansen.com
	CARTIER	cartier.com
	COPERNI	coperniparis.com
	CORGI	corgisocks.com
D	DIANA CILLIERS	@whitecubemuizenburg
	DIESEL	diesel.com
	DRIES VAN NOTEN	driesvannoten.com
G	GEISMARS	geismars.com
H	HERMÈS	hermes.com
	HOUSE OF FINN JUHL	finnjuhl.com
I	ISSEY MIYAKE	isseymiyake.com
J	J.M. WESTON	eu.jmweston.com
L	LOEWE	loewe.com
	LUKHANYO MDINGI	lukhanyomdingi.co.za
M	MAISON MARGIELA	maisonmargiela.com
	MARK KENLY DOMINO TAN	mkdtstudio.com
	MARSET	marset.com
	MATERIEL	materieltbilisi.com
N	NANUSHKA	nanushka.com
	NATURLIGVIS	naturligvis.com
	NIKE	nike.com
	NODALETO	nodaleto.com
O	OMEGA	omegawatches.com
P	POUR LUI	sanstitrepourlui.com.cn
	PRADA	prada.com
	PRIVATE POLICY	privatepolicyny.com
R	RAINS	rains.com
	ROGER DUBUIS	rogerdubuis.com
S	SELFI	selfi.co.za
	SIMONE BODMER-TURNER	simonebodmerturner.com
	STRING	stringfurniture.com
T	TIFFANY & CO.	tiffany.com
	TOTEME	toteme-studio.com
V	VENEDA CARTER	venedacarter.com
	VIPP	vipp.com
	VIVIERS	viviersstudio.com
W	WOO	discoverwoo.com
	WOOD WOOD	woodwood.com
X	XANDER ZHOU	xanderzhou.com
	XU ZHI	xuzhi.co.uk
Y	YOHJI YAMAMOTO	theshopyohjiyamamoto.com
Z	ZEGNA	zegna.com

MY FAVORITE THING

Words:
Marianne Eloise

Tattooist DR. WOO, interviewed on page 68, on the necklace that money can't buy.

There's a family-run jewelry business in Harajuku called Goro's. The original jeweler's name is Goro Takahashi and he's a legend all over Japan. He went to live in America on a [Native American] reservation and learned to make jewelry with feathers and beads. You can only buy his jewelry in Tokyo; everything is handmade, and the resale markup is astronomical.

You start with one feather and a certain material, and then you buy a new one every time you come back. Every time I went [to Tokyo] I added something, but you can only get one per visit. I just completed mine. I was very fortunate to be introduced to them and to slowly build my necklace six years ago. Even after all the years of knowing them and becoming friends with them, I still had to wait and get one bead each trip, and build it up with all the different components. The beauty of what they do is that nothing is rushed, and it doesn't matter how much money you have, you can't just buy it.

The way we move now, everything is so fast and accessible, but I love that they've kept it the same way since they started. It's very special.
—

Photo: Justin Chung